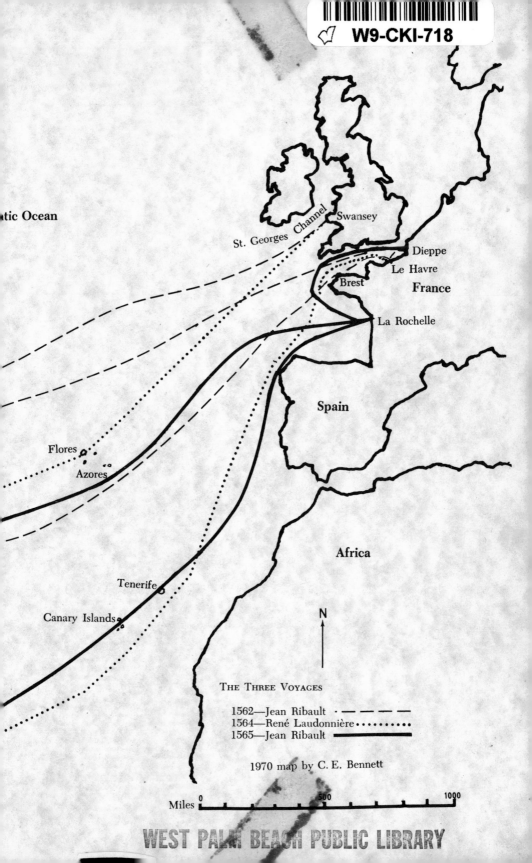

W9-CKI-718

tic Ocean

Swansey

St. Georges Channel

Dieppe

Le Havre

Brest

France

La Rochelle

Spain

Flores

Azores

Africa

Tenerife

Canary Islands

N

THE THREE VOYAGES

1562—Jean Ribault ‒ ‒ ‒
1564—René Laudonnière • • • • •
1565—Jean Ribault ⎯⎯⎯

1970 map by C. E. Bennett

Miles 0   500   1000

Portrait of René Laudonnière, painted by Roberta Bennett from a sixteenth century engraving in Crispin van de Passe, Effigies Regum Ac Principum (Colonia Agrippina, *1598*).

THREE VOYAGES

THREE VOYAGES

René Laudonnière

Translated with an introduction and notes by
Charles E. Bennett

A University of Florida Book

The University Presses of Florida
Gainesville

TYPOGRAPHY BY ROSE PRINTING COMPANY, INCORPORATED
TALLAHASSEE, FLORIDA

PRINTED BY STORTER PRINTING COMPANY, INCORPORATED
GAINESVILLE, FLORIDA

Library of Congress Cataloging in Publication Data

Laudonnière, René Goulaine de, 16th cent.
 Three voyages.

 "A University of Florida book."
 Translation of L'histoire notable de la Floride.
 Includes bibliographical references.
 1.–Florida–History–Huguenot colony, 1562–1565.
I. Bennett, Charles E., 1910–   tr. II. Title.
F314.L373 1974   917.59'1   74–12466
ISBN 0–8130–0423–3

Gratefully Dedicated
to the Memory of the late
Rembert W. Patrick

Acknowledgments

THIS BOOK would not have been produced without the generous and able assistance of a number of persons. First, Luis Arana, who is a historian for the National Park Service, was of tremendous help, particularly in the preparation of the introduction. Audrey Broward, librarian for Jacksonville University, was of great help in this work, as she has been in all of my historical efforts. Salomé Mandel of Paris contributed substantially in the research and discovered the death certificate of Laudonnière and his marriage contract. Finally, I express my gratitude to my father, the late Walter J. Bennett, who stimulated my interest in translating documents of historical interest to our country and assisted me in the first translating work I did in this field.

CHARLES E. BENNETT

Contents

Introduction xiii
Three Voyages 1
  Preface 3
  The First Voyage 17
  The Second Voyage 53
  The Third Voyage 149
Appendices
  A—Newly Discovered Portrait of Dominique de Gourgues 171
  B—*Laudonnière's Shipping Contract of 1572*
     by Jeannette Thurber Connor 173
  C—Mutual Gift Agreement between René Laudonnière
     and His Wife 181
  D—*Plant life in Sixteenth-Century Florida*
     by Tom V. Wilder 185
Notes 211
  Notes to Introduction 211
  Notes to Three Voyages 215
  Notes to Appendix B 225
Index 227

Illustrations

Map of the Three Voyages / Front endleaves
René Laudonnière / Frontispiece
Nicolas Durand, Chevalier de Villegagnon / 10
Recreation among the Timucuan Indians / 12
Gaspard de Coligny, Admiral of Châtillon / 19
A Wolf / 25
An Unidentified French Leader / 33
Charles IX / 54
Catherine de Medici / 57
René Laudonnière with Coat of Arms / 71
Chief Satouriona / 84
Map of French Explorations in America / 94
Timucuan Owl Totem / 108
Chief Outina / 118
Acorns / 126
Fort Caroline / 150
Dominique de Gourgues / Faces 171
Laudonnière's Signature / 178
Map of Mutinous Voyages from Fort Caroline / Back endleaves

xi

Introduction

AN EXPEDITION sent by the French to the New World in 1562 explored a portion of the Florida coast and established the short-lived Charlesfort settlement in present-day South Carolina. This voyage was followed in 1564 by the enterprise that resulted in the founding of Fort Caroline, on the shore of Florida's St. Johns River. Then in 1565 a third French expedition came across the Ocean Sea to reinforce the tenuous foothold on the St. Johns.

A man was present on each of these three occasions. He came as the second-in-command on the Charlesfort voyage, then commanded the force that established Fort Caroline, and finally welcomed the additional men sent to strengthen that colony. That man was René Laudonnière, and his destiny also called for his witnessing the tragic *dénouement* of the early French effort to secure a permanent place under the New World sun.

Upon his return to Europe, Laudonnière wrote an account of his participation in the aborted expeditions, which he presumably entitled "Three Voyages." A new translation of this French narrative, placed in context with contemporary events and with other French, English, and Spanish narratives about these voyages, is presented in this book. The late distinguished historian Rembert Wallace Patrick encouraged the endeavor; and Luis Arana, able historian for the National Park Service, made it possible by his substantial and scholarly guidance.

The French expedition of 1562 was led by Jean Ribault.[1] Born about 1520, Ribault held reputation as the ablest French navigator of his time. In the 1540s, Henry VIII and Edward VI of England had employed him as a consultant in navigational matters,[2] and in 1559 he had briefly represented French interests in Scotland. Gaspard de Coligny, admiral of France, had chosen him for the command.[3]

The expedition struck Florida's coast on April 30, 1562. Coasting northward, Ribault discovered the St. Johns River next day in the morning and named it the River of May. The following day he erected a stone column on a hill near the river's mouth. Engraved with the king's arms, it was meant to show French possession. Ribault then sailed north along the coast, passing nine rivers or inlets and naming most of them after rivers in France, until he reached today's Port Royal Sound.[4]

To hold the sound, Ribault built Charlesfort, which he named in honor of Charles IX of France. He also erected there another column to indicate French possession of the country. Promising to return within six months, Ribault sailed for France in June. But within short order, the fort's storeroom burned down, food became scarce, dissension broke out in the small garrison, and Charlesfort was doomed. At last the soldiers built a boat and returned to Europe.[5]

Since the beginning of the 1500s, the French had been active in exploring and attempting to settle in the New World. Possibly since 1503 Breton fishermen regularly worked off the present-day Labrador coast, which they had called the Land of the Bretons and regarded as an appurtenance of France's Brittany. Then, Francis I commissioned Giovanni Verrazano to go to the New World, and the latter reached North America's coast near 34° latitude in 1524, explored it northward to 50°, and named it New France. Moreover, France financed Jacques Cartier's visit to the Newfoundland coast in 1534, and the discovery and exploration of the St. Lawrence River and building of a fort on the estuary of St. Charles River in 1535–36. In the latter trip, Cartier held two ceremonies of taking possession, in one of which he raised a cross and the arms of France over the fort.[6]

Attempts to settle the discovered land had followed. Cartier established Charlesbourg Royal, four miles up the St. Lawrence River, in 1541. The following year, as Cartier left for France to report on the apparent wealth of the country, the Lord of Roberval took charge of the settlement. Upon his appointment as lieutenant general of Canada, an unknown country, wags in the French court had dubbed Roberval "king of Canada" and his wife "queen of Nowhere." The term *nowhere* was prophetic, for Roberval abandoned the St. Lawrence River settlement in 1543, after changing its name to France-Roy, exploring the river as Cartier had done, and failing to discover the expected material wealth of the land.[7]

The French had tried to settle next on land already held by Portugal. In 1555, Nicolas Durand, Lord of Villegagnon, built Fort Coligny in Brazil, but was wiped out five years later.[8] The Charlesfort voyage ensued.

French colonial expansion in the New World to 1562 aimed at restoring religious unity at home by engaging Protestants in breaking down the monopoly held by Spain and Portugal by virtue of Papal grant in 1493. This monopoly was a throwback to medieval canonical law and therefore had no chance of being respected in a Europe about to break out into the Renaissance and the Reformation. As early as 1510, John Maior, an English philosopher at the University of Paris, observed that the Pope had no authority to distribute the earth's surface to anyone, since the kingdom of Jesus was not of this world. Individual French fishermen were not deterred by threats of excommunication from asserting their right to travel the ocean freely. But at the same time, despite his belief that God did not create the New World for Spain and Portugal alone, Francis I had cautiously assured himself that Verrazano would not trespass upon forbidden dominions.[9]

The French believed that voyages to parts of the world not occupied by Spain did not violate the guarantee of free navigation by both Spanish and Frenchmen contained in the Treaty of Nice (1538). Indeed, the 1541 Roberval commission forbade the occupation of any country belonging to Spain or Portugal. But in the Treaty of Cateau Cambrésis (1559) the French failed to incorporate an article differentiating between regions actually occupied by the Spanish and those only claimed by them, but not settled. Instead, Spain and France agreed that the treaty would not be binding west of the Papal line of demarcation. This brought a state of continuous Franco-Spanish warfare in America, while the countries remained formally at peace in Europe.[10]

By touching at the St. Johns River and Port Royal Sound in 1562, the French trespassed upon land claimed by Spain by right of discovery, exploration, and unsuccessful attempts at settlement. Juan Ponce de León had discovered Florida in 1513, but met failure and death eight years later in his effort to colonize in the southwest of the peninsula. Likewise, Lucas Vázquez de Ayllón lost his bid to settle in today's South Carolina in 1526. But Pánfilo de Narváez (1528) and Hernando de Soto (1539) enlarged the known area of Florida through their explorations. Father Luis Cáncer de Barbastro's exclusively ecclesiastical enterprise (1549) to establish a colony on the west coast died on the sands. And Tristán de Luna's promising beginnings at Pensacola and Angel de Villafañe's search for a site in South Carolina in 1559–61 ended in withdrawal. Consequently, in 1561 Spain considered abandoning her efforts in the areas north of Mexico, a possibility quickly discarded when she found out that France had launched her 1562 expedition.[11]

Back in France from Florida, Ribault immediately fought in support of the Protestant rebels of Dieppe against the Catholic government of France. When the town fell, he fled with his English allies to England. There, he planned with Queen Elizabeth for the succour of the Frenchmen at Charlesfort. Becoming restive and uncertain as to English motives in the projected return voyage to the New World, Ribault tried to flee the country. But he was apprehended and imprisoned in the Tower of London.[12]

It was probably in jail that Ribault found time to write an account of his 1562 voyage. Although the original manuscript of this work has never been found, an English translation appeared in May 1563 under the title *The Whole and True Discouerye of Terra Florida.*[13] Ribault's prose provided such sparkling and beautiful descriptions that the book went into a second printing.[14] A facsimile reprint of the 1563 edition, with an account of the same in modern English, and a biography of Ribault by Jeannette Thurber Connor, was published in 1927 by the Florida State Historical Society.[15] More recently, to commemorate the quadricentennial of Florida's founding, Connor's volume was reprinted, with an excellent historiography by David L. Dowd, in the Floridiana Facsimile and Reprint Series.[16]

France sent René Laudonnière in 1564 to establish Fort Caroline on the banks of the St. Johns River, in present-day Jacksonville. Thus began the permanent settlement by Europeans within the present limits of the United States. Laudonnière's place and date of birth have never been clearly established. But it is believed that he was born in 1529 in the province of Poitou, in northern France, in an area called Laudonnière. In his youth he became a citizen of the port of Dieppe. He was a Protestant and a protégé, perhaps a relative, of Admiral Gaspard de Coligny. The admiral, despite the honorary character of his title, was one of the most able leaders of all time, the acknowledged head of the Huguenots (French Protestants) and the official advisor of the royal house of France. In 1561 Laudonnière, a resident of Dieppe and in command of the ship *Le Chien*, was captured by the Spanish off Catalonia. He was carrying war materials to the natives of Algiers, an act which then violated international and religious law.[17]

Life at French Fort Caroline is described in two contemporary accounts. One is the report on the voyage of Englishman John Hawkins to Africa, the West Indies, and Florida in 1564–65, written by John Sparke, Jr. During this trip Hawkins visited the French settlement from July 15 to July 28, 1565.[18] The other is a letter written by a soldier at Fort Caroline to his father in Rouen. The letter contained a sketch of the fort, the earliest printed view of a European settlement in America north of Mexico, and perhaps the first eyewitness account by a European of what is now the United States.[19] An English translation of the letter and the sketch of the fort have been republished recently.[20]

The third French expedition to Florida in 1565 resulted from Coligny's decision to reinforce Fort Caroline and transfer command there to Jean Ribault. Ribault arrived in the vicinity of Fort Caroline on August 28, but on the same day Spain's Pedro Menéndez de Avilés also reached Florida with his flotilla for the purpose of ejecting the French from the land. A devout Catholic, Menéndez had felt not only patriotic accomplishment but also religious fulfillment when he received his orders. In Florida he established St. Augustine, which became the oldest permanent settlement in what is now the United States.[21]

Apprised of the Spaniard's arrival and of his purpose, Ribault left Laudonnière at Fort Caroline and attempted to mount an attack against the Spanish ships. A hurricane wrecked the French fleet south of Matanzas Inlet. While the survivors marched northward, Menéndez cleverly marched north from his base of operations at St. Augustine and captured Fort Caroline, which he garrisoned and renamed San Mateo. Then he marched south to Matanzas Inlet, where he slew most of the Frenchmen, who in two groups came there to ask his mercy. Among those killed was Ribault, and saved were Catholics and persons with skills needed for the newly established community at St. Augustine.[22]

The accounts of the French debacle in Florida began appearing in what nowadays has been called "instant history." Among the Frenchmen who escaped from Fort Caroline on September 20 were Laudonnière, Jacques Le Moyne de Morgues, and an elderly carpenter by the name of Nicolas Le Challeux, the latter of whom had come over in the 1565 voyage.[23] All three wrote accounts of their experiences.

The Le Challeux account was the first to be published. Full of inspiring and religious fervor, it came out in 1566 and that same year went through four different French editions[24] and the first English translation.[25] The next French edition, printed thirteen years later, was part of a history of the New World,[26] as were also the first Latin edition, published in 1578,[27] and the two German editions[28] that appeared in the rest of the continent.

The 1566 English translation of Le Challeux's account is less awkward for the modern reader than the 1587 English translation of Laudonnière's narrative. Even in such ancient English, the carpenter's account comes through with vitality and charm. Yet some words have changed meaning through the years, and we are indebted to Stefan Lorant for a modernized English version.[29]

Interrupting the chronology in the appearance of the accounts dealing with the loss of Fort Caroline, let us dispose of the Le Moyne narrative before coming to that of Laudonnière. Le Moyne had been one of the 1564 settlers of Fort Caroline, and after his flight from there he settled in England. He gathered the events which he saw and knew about from his presence at Fort Caroline and from information he had learned from others, principally from Laudonnière. Le Moyne wrote in more detail than the other two chroniclers, and drew very instructive and ably done illustrations. His narrative, the drawings, and a map were turned over to Theodore de Bry by Le Moyne's widow. De Bry had the manuscript translated into Latin, the drawings and map made into engravings, and the whole published in 1591.[30] This first appearance was shortly followed the same year by a German edition.[31]

The first translation into English of the Le Moyne narrative, done by Fred B. Perkins, was not published until 1875.[32] The Perkins translation and reproductions of all the De Bry engravings, as colored by an unknown artist of the sixteenth century, have again been made available recently.[33] A new English translation from the Latin and all forty-two of Le Moyne's drawings and maps from De Bry had appeared a score of years earlier.[34] Curiously enough, Le Moyne's original manuscript, which he may have written in French or English, has never been discovered.

After the fall of Fort Caroline, René Laudonnière succeeded in returning to Europe. He reached England late in 1565 and stayed there until he left for France to report personally to King Charles IX in March 1566. During this sojourn Laudonnière wrote, as is apparent from the text, the delightful account of his adventures in Florida in 1562, 1564, and 1565. The narrative is primarily a carefully written, official communication apparently for the eyes only of Charles or perhaps Admiral Coligny.

Only Laudonnière was present on all three voyages, and thus he rightly became their chief historian. None of the other three major eyewitness accounts by Frenchmen dealing with these expeditions has the accuracy of detail, the broad scope, the attractive composition, or the historical significance of Laudonnière's narrative. Not only does it cover the whole period of the three voyages, as witnessed by a participant, but it also shows a more scientific interest in things observed in the New World. Besides history, the chronicle is also exceedingly well-recorded geography and anthropology.

Laudonnière's writing is a splendid factual account of what happened, told with considerable candor and accuracy. After reciting the dangers of undermanned foreign expeditions (and observing this in the context of the experience at Fort Caroline), he concluded that "all this the French have proved true and to my regret in the last few days." The latter words clearly show that Laudonnière began writing before 1565 had ended.

The somewhat defensive attitude of some portions of Laudonnière's writing was apparently to vindicate his leadership. But the necessity is not obvious because Ribault, not Laudonnière, was in command in Fort Caroline at the time of the disaster which returned Florida to Spain in 1565.

Laudonnière's account deserves to stand alone. It towers above the work of Ribault, Le Challeux, and Le Moyne. It earned for him a great place as a historian and a geographer. Laudonnière apparently never sought to publish his writing at a time in history when much less readable stories of foreign adventure were at a premium with the publishers.

Laudonnière's narrative, entitled "Three Voyages," was originally published in *L'Histoire notable de la Florida, située ès Indes Occidentales*, which appeared in 1586, twelve years after his death.[35] The title may have been on the original manuscript, which is not now known to survive. Although the account has been cited without exception as *L'histoire notable . . .* this book also contained the story of the 1568 voyage of Dominique de Gourgues, which certainly was not written by Laudonnière. The original work was reprinted in 1853.[36] Laudonnière's original manuscript was discovered by Richard Hakluyt, who published the first English translation of the narrative in 1587.[37] This translation is available in reprints, some recent.[38]

The Hakluyt translation is interesting to readers who appreciate the charm of old English, but it has definite limitations. It is inaccurate in some specific and significant matters. It says, for instance, that there were twenty-six men left behind in the Charlesfort settlement of 1562, while Laudonnière's original statement shows the figure to be twenty-eight. Similarly, the Hakluyt translation says in its preface that the French came in 1561, while Laudonnière originally and correctly says 1562. Furthermore, the structure of Hakluyt's sentences, when taken with the use of archaic words, makes the reading very difficult and sometimes misleading. Hakluyt also puts some sentences out of place and adds some matters not in the original text.

There is still an unpublished English translation of the Laudonnière account. It was done in the 1930s by translators with the Writers' Project of the federal Works Progress Administration. Apparently made from the account in the 1853 French edition, it could also be a rework of the 1587 translation. When the unpublished translation, a typescript of which is at Fort Caroline National Memorial, is compared with the original French text, some omissions are found.

As would be expected, the French debacle at Fort Caroline is also covered in several Spanish sources. For instance, Gonzalo Solís de Merás, brother-in-law of Menéndez and a participant in the 1565 Spanish expedition, wrote in 1567 a *Memorial* of the events concerning the conquest of French Florida. It was not published in any form until it was partially used by Andrés González de Barcia Carballido y Zúñiga,[39] and it was not published in its entirely for the first time until 1893.[40] The *Memorial* was first translated into English by Jeannette Thurber Connor in this present century.[41] More recently, Connor's work was given a facsimile reproduction with an excellent historiographical introduction by Lyle N. McAlister.[42]

A second major Spanish contemporary source was the narrative of Francisco López de Mendoza Grajales, chaplain of the 1565 expedition. This was first published in a French translation.[43] It was first published in Spanish as part of a forty-two-volume work of printed manuscripts which appeared between 1864 and 1884.[44] Ruidíaz published it in Spanish again in 1893.[45] The first English translation, by B. F. French, appeared in 1875,[46] followed many years later by publication of a second translation.[47] There is a more recent appearance in English of the Father López narrative.[48]

The third major contemporary account in Spanish was a biography of Menéndez written in 1568 by Bartolomé Barrientos, a professor at the University of Salamanca. It was first published as "Vida y hechos de Pero Menéndez de Avilés,"[49] but it was not until very recently that at last this account was translated into English, by Anthony Kerrigan. The translation was published together with a facsimile reproduction of the Barrientos text by the University of Florida Press.[50]

After his return to France and his appearance before the king at Moulins, Laudonnière continued to pursue his profession as a navigator. For a time he was so employed by the Cardinal of Bourbon (Archbishop of Rouen), sailing in American waters on the 120-ton *Countess Testu*, the royal arsenals furnishing his artillery. Despite his employment in the service of a Catholic leader, he firmly remained Protestant.[51]

In 1572 Laudonnière, then a resident of Paris, agreed to command a nautical enterprise to America, and unwittingly saved his own life. He was preparing to go to sea and was distant from the chief areas of danger on August 24, when the St. Bartholomew's Day massacre took place. On this occasion, his intimate friend and sponsor, Coligny, and many thousands of the Huguenot community were slaughtered, all with the approval of Charles IX and his mother, Catherine de Medici. The sailing contract which originated this voyage is still preserved. It is dated May 16, 1572, and is signed by Laudonnière. The only other known signature of Laudonnière is on a receipt, dated November 1573, acknowledging payment from the treasurer of France for services rendered. The receipt's endorsement describes Laudonnière as "The Captain of the Western Fleet."[52]

Laudonnière's last days were spent in Saint-Germain-en-Laye, near Paris, and here he died on Saturday, July 24, 1574. He was buried on Sunday and services for him were held on Monday. In the original French, the death notice reads as follows: "Le samedi vingt quatrième, mourust Monsieur le Capitaine de Laudonnière, et fust inhumé le dimanche, et le lundy ensuyvant fust faict son service."[53] Coincidentally and ironically, Charles IX and Pedro Menéndez also died in 1574.

Laudonnière's right to fame rests chiefly on his leading the expedition that began the permanent European settlement of present-day United States. He founded the colony of Fort Caroline in 1564 and governed it until the latter part of 1565, when the leadership was transferred, just prior to the conquest by the Spanish, to Jean Ribault. Next, he deserves great credit for his extremely able and accurate writing of the account that is freshly translated in this book. It merits for him a high place among geographers and historians. Finally, in an age of great navigators he was one of the most able. In this latter capacity he served Catherine de Medici, Charles IX, Francis I, Francis II, and Henry II, all of them sovereigns of France.

THREE VOYAGES

Preface

In which are described the customs and manner of living of the Indians who inhabit the valley of the River of May in Florida

IN MY OPINION there are two reasons which have principally stimulated man to travel to foreign lands, both in the past and in the present. The first has been a normal desire to discover the means for a better life, fully and easily achieved whether by totally quitting the native land to live in a better one, or by making frequent trips of discovery to bring back things greatly desired or required in the homeland. The other reason for peoples' going to distant lands has been the population explosion which has made it impossible for people to stay in their native lands.[1] So they have spilled over into neighboring countries and have more often than not traveled to even more distant areas.

In this way the North, fertile father of a host of people, has exported here and there its most courageous people, and has populated many countries. This is the reason most European nations owe their origin to this area. On the other hand, the more southerly regions, which are relatively unproductive because of controlling high temperatures, have had no need to send their people away and have often been forced to receive other people, more often by combat than by friendship. All Africa, Spain, and Italy can testify to this. They were never so crowded with people that they had to send them abroad, as Scythia, Norway, Gothia, and France had to do. The descendants of these countries still dwell not only in Italy, Spain, and Africa, but also in beautiful Asia.

I find that the Romans added another to these two principal reasons for foreign settlement. They were anxious to establish their laws, customs, and religion in the areas which they conquered. Their senate often sent out expeditions of people to form colonies. In this way they sought to make their name immortal. But they depopulated their own country in a way that was more harmful than helpful in their quest for world government. This was so because their colonies were overrun by foreign people who finally destroyed the empire. The banks of the Rhine River are still red, and those of the Danube just as bloody, and our France was made slippery by all the blood that they spilled.

These, then, are the results and wages of all those who, driven by tyrannical and Roman ambition, try to overcome foreigners. These results, I say, are contrary to the rewards received by those who are only interested in the public good, that is, in the universal well-being of all people, and try to bring unity one with the other, more by foreign commerce and communications than by military measures, except when these foreigners do not want to pay attention to their obligations which are so beneficial to them.

So, monarchs have sent out enterprising persons to establish themselves in distant lands to make a profit, to civilize the countryside, and, if possible, to bring the local inhabitants to the true knowledge of God. These are commendable objectives quite foreign to tyrannical and cruel conquest. And so they have always nurtured enterprises and bit by bit gained the hearts of those conquered or won over by other means.

From all of this we can see that it is often good, even wise, to send out people to discover the good things and the products of strange countries; but always in a way that creates no weakness in the homeland. Also those sent out should be in numbers so sufficient that they will not be defeated by those in the foreign lands who may seek to ambush them and to defeat them. All of this the French have proved true and to my great regret in the last few days. It was not possible to prevent this under the circumstances of the weather, the number of available men, and the omitted favors that one would have a right to expect from a faithful and Christian ally who fought against us. All of this I intend to discuss in this account which I am writing, with a truthfulness so evident that my king will be satisfied in part with the diligence that I have exerted in his service; and so that my enemies will have no place to hide in their untruths. But before beginning I will briefly describe the situation and the nature of the land to which we sailed and in which we have lived from 1562 until 1565, so that the things which I write about can be more easily understood.

That part of the earth which today we call the fourth part of the world, or America, or rather West India, was not known to our ancestors because of its remoteness. Similarly, the Western Islands[2] and the Fortunate Islands[3] were not discovered until modern times. However, some people have claimed that they were discovered in the days of Augustus Caesar and that Virgil made mention of them in the sixth book of his *Aeneid* when he said there was a land over there among the stars, a year's voyage away according to the sun, there at the place where Atlas supported the pole upon his shoulders. Nevertheless, it is easy to see that he did not intend to talk about this land since he was the only one who wrote of it during his time and even for a thousand years thereafter. Christopher Columbus first of all went to this land in 1492. Five years afterwards Americus went there by order of the king of Castile and gave it his own name. Forever afterwards it was called America. Fortunately this man was very knowledgeable in the art of navigation and in astronomy, and as a result he discovered many lands unknown to earlier geographers. Some people also call this land Brazil and Papegalli. According to Postel it stretches from one pole to the other, except at the Straits of Magellan, and there reaches 52 degrees beyond the equator.

To better describe America, I will divide it into three principal parts. The land which is toward the Arctic, or the north, is called New France because even as early as 1524 Jean Verrazano, a Florentine, was sent to these new lands by Francis I and his mother, the regent. He landed there and explored the entire coast which has since been known as the Tropic of Cancer, from the 28th degree to the 50th and even farther north. He placed the flag there and the coat-of-arms of the king of France, so that even the Spanish when they came afterwards called the country French. The land stretches then from 25 degrees in latitude to 54 degrees toward the north and in longitude from 210 degrees to 330 degrees. The eastern part of this land is now called Norumberge. This begins at the Bay of Gamas[4] which separates it from the Isle of Canada, where Robert Val and Jacques Cartier went in 1535. There are many islands in that area and among them is Labrador which stretches toward Greenland. In the western part there are many known areas such as the regions of Quivira, Cevola, Astatlan, and Terlichichimici. The southern part is called Florida because it was discovered on the feast day of Pasques Flories. The northern part is absolutely unknown.

The second general part of America is called New Spain. It extends to the 9th degree from the Tropic of Cancer at the 25th degree. In it is situated the city of Themistitan, and it has many regional areas and many islands called the Antilles. The most important and well known of these islands are Hispaniola and Isabella, and there are many others. All of this land together with the Gulf of Mexico and all of the said islands do not exceed 70 degrees in longitude, to wit: from 240 up to 310. It is an area as long and as narrow as Italy.

The third part of America is called Peru. It is very large and extends in latitude from the 10th degree up to 55 degrees from the equator and on to the Straits of Magellan. It is shaped like an egg and is well known on all coasts. Its largest portion covers 60 degrees; and from there it grows narrower and narrower toward both ends. In one part of this land Villegagnon lived, right under the Tropic of Capricorn. He named it Antarctic France because it approaches the Antarctic pole, just as our land approaches the Arctic pole.

New France is about as large as all Europe. The most known and inhabited part of it is Florida, where so many Frenchmen have made visits at various times that it is now the best known country in this part of New France. The cape of this area is a long piece of land extending into the sea about 100 leagues running straight south. Right over against it at a distance of 25 leagues sits the island of Cuba, sometimes called Isabella. Towards the east are the islands of Bahama and Lucaye, and toward the west there is the Gulf of Mexico. The country is flat and divided by many rivers, and it is therefore moist. It is sandy toward the seashores. Many pines grow there, and there are no kernels in the cones they bear.

The woods are full of oak, walnut, black cherry, mulberry, gum and chestnut trees, which are not exactly the same as those in France. There are many cedars, cypress, magnolia,⁵ palm, and holly trees; and wild vines climb among the trees and bear good grapes. There is a type of medlar,⁶ and the fruit of it is better and bigger than that of France. There are also plum trees which bear beautiful but not very good fruit. There are raspberries and a little berry which we call the blueberry, very good to eat. In that country a kind of root grows which they call *hassez,* and in necessity they can make bread from it.[7]

The animals which are best known in that area are deer, stags, goats, does, bears, panthers, bobcats, wildcats, several kinds of wolves, wild dogs, hares, rabbits, Indian chickens [turkeys], partridges, parrots,[8] pigeons,[9] doves, turtledoves, blackbirds, crows, hawks, falcons, shrikes, herons, cranes, storks, wild geese, ducks, cormorants, white, red, black, and gray herns, and an infinite variety of game. There are also so many crocodiles that men in swimming are often attacked by them.[10] There are many types of snakes and a certain species of animal which differs very little from the lion of Africa.[11]

Among the Indians there are found quantities of gold and silver, which they say come from the ships which have been wrecked on the coast. They trade among one another in these metals. What makes me believe their story is that on the coast toward the cape where the ships are usually sunk there is much more silver among them than on the northern coast. They say nevertheless that in the Appalachian Mountains there are copper mines, which I believe to be gold.[12]

There are also in this land the chinaroot tree,[13] which is very good medicine against syphilis, and large quantities of berries and herbs from which they make very good dyes and paints of all colors.[14] In fact the Indians, who love to paint their skins, know how to use these dyes very well.

The men are olive in color, large of body, handsome, well proportioned, and without deformities. They cover their loins with well-cured deer skins. Most of

Nicolas Durand, Chevalier de Villegagnon, French navy commander and leader of the Huguenot expedition and settlement in Brazil in the 1550s, the drawing being owned by Mr. and Mrs. Winslow Ames.

them ornament their bodies, arms, and thighs with handsome designs. The ornamentation is in permanent color because it is pricked into the skin. Their hair is very black and extends to their hips in length. However, they truss it up in a very becoming manner.

They are great dissemblers and deceivers. Brave in spirit, they fight well. Their only weapons are bows and arrows, and they make the string for their bows from the gut of a stag or from stag skin. They know how to tan this just as well as the French do, and, moreover, in different colors. They make their arrowheads from the teeth of fish and from stones which they cleverly fashion. They exercise their young men to become excellent runners, and they give prizes to those who have the greatest endurance. They often practice at archery. They play ball in the following fashion: They use a tree standing in an open place, a tree eight or nine armlengths in height. At the top of the tree there is a square made from wood strips, and the scorer is the one who hits the square. They also take great pleasure in hunting and fishing.

The kings make wars among themselves, always by surprise attack. They kill every male enemy they can. Then they cut the skin off their heads to preserve the hair, and carry this back on their triumphant homeward journeys. They spare the enemy women and children, feed them, and retain them permanently among themselves. On returning from war, they gather all their subjects together in a celebration of merrymaking for three days and three nights, dancing and singing. They even make the old women dance while holding the enemy scalps in their hands. As the Indians dance, they sing praises to the sun, attributing

Recreation among the Tumucuan Indians, being the thirty-sixth of the engravings of Jacques Le Moyne de Morgues in his book Brevis Narratio *(Frankfort, deBry, 1591).*

to the sun the honor of their victory. They have no knowledge of God or of any religion except that which appears to them, such as the sun and the moon.

They have their priests in whom they have great faith because they are able magicians, diviners, and invokers of devils. These priests are their doctors and surgeons. The priests always carry with them a bag of herbs and drugs[15] to administer to the sick who, for the most part, are syphilitic on account of their great love for the women and maidens whom they call daughters of the sun. Yet some of the Indians are Sodomites.

Each man is married to one woman. The king is permitted to have two or three wives, but his first wife is the only one recognized as queen, and only her children inherit the property and authority of the father. The women do all the housework. The husband does not live with his wife when he knows her to be pregnant, and does not eat anything the wife touches while she is in this condition. There are in this country a large number of hermaphrodites[16] who do all the heaviest labor and bear the victuals when the group go to war. They paint their faces and fluff out their hair with feathers in order to make themselves as repulsive as possible. The foods which they carry are bread, honey, and flour made of corn that has been parched in the fire. This remains fresh a long time. Sometimes they also carry smoked fish.

In necessity they eat a thousand unattractive things, even swallowing charcoal and putting earth in their mush.

When the Indians go to war, their king goes first with a mace in one hand and his bow in the other, his quiver full of arrows. All his soldiers follow him with their bows and arrows, yelling and screaming in combat.

The men do nothing without assembling and counseling together thoroughly before arriving at a decision. They meet together every morning in the great public house where the king is and where he sits on a seat higher than all the others. There each, one after the other, comes and salutes him. The older ones begin the salutations by raising both hands twice on a level with their faces, saying, "Ha, he, ya, ha, ha." The others respond, "Ha, ha." In this way they all salute and take seats all around in the house. If there is business to transact, the king calls the priests and also the elders and asks their advice. Then he orders some cassena.[17] This is a drink made from the leaves of a certain tree, and it is drunk very hot. The king drinks first and then they all drink, one after the other, from the vessel, which holds about a quart by Paris measure. They esteem this beverage so much that no one can drink of it in this assembly if he has not already proven himself to be a warrior. Moreover, this drink makes them break out in a very heavy sweat; and when the sweat has passed away, they do not hunger or thirst for twenty-four hours thereafter.

When a king dies, they bury him very solemnly, and on his grave they put the cup from which he usually drank. All about the grave they stick many arrows, and there are three days and three nights of continuous fasting and lamentation. All the kings who are friends of the departed king mourn in the same manner. As testimony of their friendship to the deceased, they cut off more than half their hair, men and women alike. For a period of six months certain women are delegated to mourn the death of the king, crying out in a loud voice three times each day, morning, noon, and night. All the worldly goods of the king are put in his house, which is then set on fire so that nothing of his will ever be seen again. They do the same thing for their priests; and a priest's body is put in the house before it is set afire.

The Indians sow their corn twice a year, in March and June, replanting the same soil. This corn, from the time it is sown until the time it is harvested, is in the ground about three months, and the land is allowed to rest during the other six months of the year.[18] They also gather good pumpkins and very good beans. They do not fertilize their ground except when they start to sow it. Then they set the weeds on fire, which have been growing for six months, and burn them all away. They work the ground with a wooden hoe, such as is used in France in digging around vines. They plant two grains of corn together. When the land is to be sown, the king commands one of his men to assemble his subjects every day to labor, during which time the king causes the supply of the drink already mentioned to be made for them. In the harvest season all of the grain is carried into the public house and distributed to each according to his quality or rank. They do not sow any more than they feel is necessary for a period of six months, scarcely that.

During the winter they retire for three or four months into the woods where they make little huts of palm leaves and live on acorns, fish which they catch, oysters, deer, turkeys, and other animals which they hunt. They eat all their meat broiled over charcoal or smoked. They eat the flesh of crocodiles and, in fact, it is good and white. However it has a musky smell. We have often eaten it with them.

When they become sick and have a pain, their custom is, instead of letting blood flow as we do, to have their physicians suck the place of the pain until the blood comes forth.

The women are built along the same lines as the men, large, tall, and of the same color, painted just like the men; however, when they are born they are not so olive-colored and are much whiter. The principal cause of this color is the oil with which they rub themselves, and they do this for a certain ceremony which I could not learn about. Their color comes also from the sun which shines hot upon their bodies. The agility of the women is so great that they can swim a river of great size, holding their infants on one arm, and then climb nimbly among the highest trees in the countryside.

There you have a brief description of the country and of the nature and customs of the inhabitants. This I have been happy to write about before entering into the thread of my story. In this way the reader will be better prepared to understand what I am going to tell about.

The First Voyage
of the French to Florida,
Made in 1562 by
Captain Jean Ribault

THE ADMIRAL of Châtillon [Coligny], a nobleman more anxious for the public good than for his own, having learned of the desire of his king to explore new lands, set about promptly to equip the vessels and enlist the proper men for such an enterprise. Among these was Captain Jean Ribault, a true expert in marine affairs. Ribault, having received his orders, put to sea on February 18, 1562. He had only two ships of the king, but he was well supplied with gentlemen, of whom I was one, and with experienced soldiers with whom it would be possible to achieve notable and memorable deeds.

After having navigated for about two months, carefully evading the Spanish route, Ribault made port in New France, setting foot near a cape or headland. It was not a high place because the coast is flat there, with its elevation only in trees. Upon his arrival he called it Cape François, in honor of our country. This cape is about 30° from the equator.[19]

Cruising from this place northward, he discovered a very large and beautiful river, which prompted him to drop anchor so that he could reconnoiter the place early on the following morning. He did this at daybreak, accompanied by Captain Fiquinville and other soldiers from his ship. When he arrived at the river bank, right away he saw many male and female Indians who had come to this place to receive the Frenchmen with gentleness and kindness. This was emphasized by the speech of their king and by the presentation of chamois skins to our captain. On the following day Captain Ribault erected a column of hard stone[20] on the banks of this river,[21] not far from the mouth of the river and on a little sandy knoll. The coat of arms of France was carved upon it.

This done, he embarked again to continue the survey of the northern coast as he had planned. After navigating a bit, he landed on the other side of the river and commanded everyone, in the presence of the Indians who purposefully waited on him there, to thank God that He had by His grace directed the French people to this strange land without danger or accident. The Indians, who had listened attentively, thinking, I suppose, that we were worshiping the sun because we always had our eyes lifted up to Heaven, rose up when the prayers were ended and came to salute Captain Jean Ribault. They asked to introduce their king, who had not arisen as they had done but

Gaspard de Coligny, Admiral of France, drawing from the school of François Clouet, from the collections of the Library of Congress.

had remained seated on green magnolia and palmetto leaves. The captain went forward and sat down near him and listened to his long discourse; but with little pleasure because he could not understand the language, much less the meaning.

At the leave-taking the king gave the captain a plume of egret feathers, dyed red, and a basket made from palm fiber, very artfully constructed, together with a great skin drawn upon and painted with pictures of various wild beasts, so vividly represented that they seemed almost alive. The captain, wishing not to appear ungrateful, gave him some little silver-plated bracelets, a sickle, a mirror, and some knives. The king indicated that he was very happy and fully satisfied. The better part of the day having passed in the visit with the Indians, the captain embarked on his ship to go over to the other side of the river. The king showed himself to be very displeased about this; nevertheless, not being able to prevent it, the king ordered us to be provided with fish, which was done speedily. They went to their weirs, or enclosures, made out of reeds like a maze, and loaded us up with trout, mullet, flounder, turbot, and a multitude of other species which are different from ours. This done, we entered our boats again and went toward the other shore.

Before we landed, we were greeted by another group of Indians who came out into the water up to their armpits, bringing us little baskets full of corn and freshly washed red and white mulberries. Others offered themselves to bear us to the shore. When we landed, we saw their king seated on a heap of cedar and magnolia boughs under a little arbor near the river bank. He was attended by two of his sons, each of great handsomeness and of strong body, and also by a band of Indians who had all their bows and bundles of arrows in excellent shape. The two sons received our captain graciously, but their father, the king, showed great solemnness and did nothing but slightly move his head. When the captain came up to salute him, the king retained such a grave dignity that he seemed indeed to warrant the title of king. The captain did not know how to judge this deportment and thought that the king might be jealous because we went first to the other side of the river, or perhaps that he was not very happy about the stone marker that we had erected. Not knowing anything else to do, we indicated by signs that we had come from a great distance on purpose to see him and to make known the friendship that we desired. In confirmation of this, Ribault took from a small chest a few trinkets, such as gilt- and silver-plated bracelets, and presented them to the king and gave a few others to his sons. This finally put the king in an amiable mood toward the captain and us.

After these indications of good will we walked through the woods, hoping to discover something new. We observed large numbers of white and red mulberries, and on the tops of these many silkworms. Following our course, we discovered a beautiful and large meadow interlaced with marshes, and then the wet condition of the ground caused us to turn back. The king was no longer present when we returned because he had retired to his home. So we went into our small

boats to return to our ships. On our arrival we called
this river the River of May because we had discovered
it on May 1.

Shortly after we had returned to our ships, anchors
were raised and sails unfurled for further exploration
along the coast, where we soon discovered another
beautiful river which the captain wished to reconnoiter. Having investigated that area with the king
and the people there, he named it the Seine River
because it resembled the Seine River in France.[22] We
left the river valley to go back to our ships, and on
arriving, we let loose our sails in a northward journey
to discover the shape of the coast.

We had not gone far when we discovered another
beautiful river, and we dropped anchor to investigate
it. Trimming out two boats for the reconnaissance, we
discovered an island and a king, as affable as the others.
We named this river the Somme River.[23] From there
we sailed about six leagues where we discovered
another river, explored it, and named it the Loire
River.[24] Subsequently we discovered five others, the
first of which we called the Charente,[25] the second
Garonne,[26] the third Gironde,[27] the fourth Belle,[28] and
the fifth Grande.[29] All of these river valleys and their
contents were reconnoitered by us. In less than sixty
leagues we had seen many notable things along nine
rivers.

Nevertheless, not being fully satisfied, we sailed
yet farther northward, following a course that could
bring us to the Jordan River, one of the best of the
north land.[30] As we followed this course, great fogs
and heavy storms came, forcing us to abandon the coast
and to sail out into the open seas. This caused us to

lose sight of our barques for one day and one night. The next morning at daybreak when the weather became normal and the sea calmer, we discovered a river which we called Belle à Veoir.[31] After we had sailed three or four leagues, we caught sight of our barques, which came straight toward us. At their arrival they reported to the captain that during the bad weather and the fog they had drawn back into a large river, exceeding the others in size and beauty. The captain was very happy about this because the primary purpose now was to find a haven to harbor his ships and to refresh ourselves for a space of time.

Pursuing this course, we arrived astraddle the river which we called Port Royal because of its beauty and grandeur.[32] We lowered sails and dropped anchor in ten fathoms of water. The depth of the water is so great there, where the sea begins to flow, that the largest ships of France, yes the galleons of Venice, could enter there.

Being anchored, the captain landed with some of his soldiers. He was the first to land and found a place so pleasant that it was beyond comparison. It was completely covered with numerous tall oaks and cedars, and underneath them there were gums of such good aroma that they alone would have made the place most attractive.[33] Strolling under the branches, we saw many turkeys flying through the forest, and some red and grey partridges, somewhat different from ours, chiefly in their large size. We also observed deer running through the woods, and some bears, wolves, panthers, and many other types of animals not known to us. Being pleased with this place, we went fishing there with our seine and took an unusually large number of fish. Among others, we took a species which we call saillicoques.[34] They are none other than crayfish, and two draggings of the net were enough to feed all the company of our two ships for a whole day.

The river mouth is at least three French leagues wide. It is divided into two great arms, one running west and the other north. I believe that the arm which stretches to the north extends to the Jordan River and that the other goes into the sea, according to the information coming to us from those who lived in this place. These two arms of the river cover two great leagues. In the midst of these there is an island which points toward the opening of the great river and on this there were many sorts of strange animals. Among them there were large numbers of ordinary animals of excellent quality. It was a beautiful thing to see. Around there, everywhere, there were palm trees and many other kinds of trees, and flowers and fruit with rare shapes and attractive perfumes.

Seeing the night approach and the captain thinking about going back to the ship, we asked that he allow us to spend the night in this place. In our absence the pilots and master mariners had advised the captain that the ship should come farther up the river to prevent injuries from the winds that might spring up, since we were so near to the mouth of the river. So for this reason the captain sent for us, and arriving at our ships again, we sailed up the river three leagues and dropped anchor.

A little while afterwards, Jean Ribault, accompanied by a substantial number of soldiers, embarked to navigate the western branch of the river and to seek

Latinè Lvpvs.   Gallicè Lovp.

German. VVolf.   Anglicè VVolfe.

A wolf, a woodcut from Jacques Le Moyne de Morgues, La Clef des Champs (London, Blackfriars, 1586).

out its advantages. Having traveled a good twelve leagues, we observed a band of Indians who, on seeing our barques, became so frightened that they fled into the woods, leaving behind them a young wolf that they were turning on a spit. For this reason we called this place Cape Wolf.[35] Proceeding farther, we found another stream, which flowed toward the east. The captain decided to sail up this, abandoning the larger river. Shortly afterward, we observed many Indians, men and women, half hidden in the woods. At first they were in doubt about our intentions and were fearful, but later on they were reassured. The captain showed them certain trading merchandise, and from this they could understand that he meant them no harm. They made a sign that we should come to land. This we did, for we did not want to refuse them.

Upon our coming ashore, some of them came to salute our general according to their native customs. Some gave him deerskins, others little baskets, and a few presented pearls to him, but not in large quantities. Then they began to build a shelter in this place to shade us from the heat of the sun; but we really did not wish to stay there any longer. The captain thanked them for their kindness and gave them each a present. He pleased them so much that when he started to leave, our sudden departure was not well accepted by them. Knowing him to be so generous, they wanted him to stay a little while longer and sought by every possible means to give him an occasion to stay, showing him by signs that should he stay just one day they could advise a great Indian king who had pearls in abundance and silver also, which would be presented to the captain when the king arrived.

They said further that in the meanwhile we could pass the time until the great king came by visiting their houses and by them showing us some fun in archery and deer hunting. They pleaded with the captain not to deny them their request.

Nevertheless we returned to the ships. After having been there one night, the captain ordered us to load into a small boat a pillar of hard stone fashioned like a column, on which was cut the coat of arms of the king of France.[36] He told us it was to be planted in the best place that we could find. This being ordered, we embarked and sailed three leagues toward the west. There we discovered a little river up which we navigated until at the end we found ourselves returning to the main current, making a little island separated from the high land. We landed on the island and planted the stone pillar there upon a hill,[37] in a spot with an open view near a lake with a half fathom of very good fresh water. This was in accord with the order of the captain, for it was indeed a beautiful and pleasant place. On the island we saw two large deer exceeding in size all those we had ever seen before, and we might easily have killed them with our guns if the captain had not forbidden us to do so because of their great beauty and size.

Before leaving, we named the little river around the island the Liborne River.[38] Then we embarked to look over another island which was not far from the first. On landing we found nothing but tall cedars, the most beautiful that we had seen in this country. So we called this the Isle of Cedars,[39] and we re-embarked to return to our vessel.

Several days afterwards, Jean Ribault decided to

return among the Indians who inhabited the west arm of the river and to take with him a large number of soldiers. His plan was to capture two Indians of that place and to take them back to France, as the queen had commanded him. Having arrived at this conclusion, we returned to the same place where we had first found the Indians, and we took two Indians by permission of their king. Thinking that they were more favored than the rest, they thought themselves very fortunate to be with us; but seeing that we were not going to land but stayed in the full stream of the river, they became alarmed and tried to leap into the water. Being such good swimmers, they could have been quickly away and lost in the forest. Knowing their feelings, we watched them carefully and sought to appease them. We did everything possible, giving them things they liked the most. But they disdained to accept and returned the things which they had already received, thinking by this that we would feel obliged to free them.

Knowing finally that nothing was going to do any good, they asked for the rejected things to be returned. We gave these things back right away, and then they joined each other in singing softly and sweetly in a way that made us think that they lamented the absence of their friends. They continued the singing all night long without stopping. During this time we were forced to remain at anchor because the tide was running against us, but we set sail the next morning and returned to the ships.

Upon arriving, each of us made an effort to please the two Indians and to be as pleasant as possible so that they would know of our desire to become better friends in the future. We gave them something to eat, but they refused and told us that before eating they were accustomed to wash their faces and then to wait until the setting of the sun. This is a ceremony among all the Indians in New France. Later they were constrained to forget their superstitions and to accommodate themselves to our customs, but it was all somewhat strange to them at first. They finally became a little more at ease, and then they tried to start a thousand conversations and were very sorry indeed that we could not understand them. In a few days they began to show me real affection, and it seemed that they would prefer death from hunger or thirst to taking food from anyone's hands but mine.

Observing such a friendly attitude on their part, I tried to learn some of the Indian terms, showing them things that I wished to name in their language. They were very happy to instruct me; and knowing of the desire that I had to learn their language, they invited me to ask them anything. So by putting in writing the terms and locations of Indian things, I came to understand the greater part of their conversations. Every day, without fail, they told me that they would be even kinder to me if we would return to their homes. They said that they would give me every pleasure that I could desire, such as hunting or seeing their secret feast ceremonies which they called "Toya." They observe this feast as religiously as we do our Sabbath.

They told me that they would let me meet Chiquola, the great lord of that territory, who stands a foot and a half taller than they. They informed me that he inhabited a very spacious area with a high enclosure, but I could not learn what it was made of. As far as I can judge, this place they spoke of is a very large city. They told me that inside the enclosure there are many houses of substantial height, having in them large numbers of men like themselves, and that they had no concern for gold, silver, or pearls because they had them in great abundance.[40] I began to show them the parts of the heavens in order to find out where those people lived. One of them instantly made it known that they lived in the north, which makes me think that it was on the Jordan River.

This reminded me that in the reign of Emperor Charles V some Spanish inhabitants of Santo Domingo had made a trip to capture slaves to work in the mines and had cleverly stolen away about forty of the inhabitants of this river valley, planning to carry them back to New Spain. But their effort was fruitless, because the captives all died of hunger, except one. He was brought to the Emperor, who caused him to be baptized and gave him his own name. He called him Charles of Chiquola because he talked so much about his love for his King Chiquola. Likewise, he reported consistently that Chiquola lived within a very great enclosure. Besides this corroboration, those who were left behind on the first expedition told me that the Indians had let them know by signs that farther inland toward the north there was a great enclosure and many beautiful houses, among which Chiquola lived.

But not to get off the subject, I return to the Indian who took such great pleasure in telling me of Chiquola that not a single day passed without his recounting something unusual about the king. After the Indians had stayed a while on our ships, they began to be very depressed and would not talk about anything but returning home. I told them that the captain planned to send them back home again, but that he first wanted to give them some apparel. A few days later this was given to them. But seeing that no one gave them license to leave, they resolved to escape during the night, take a little boat that we had, and by the help of the tide find their way back to their homes and safety. They carried out the plan and left behind all the clothing that the captain had given them, taking nothing except that which belonged to them. This showed clearly that they were men of good character. The captain was not particularly disturbed at their departure, since they had received nothing but good treatment and thus they would bring no ill will toward France.

Captain Ribault, observing the singular beauty of this river, strongly wished to inspire some of the men to inhabit the area, knowing full well that this would be of great importance in the service of the king and to the benefit of the French nation. To carry out this thought, he ordered the anchors raised and everything set in order to return to the mouth of the river. If the winds were found favorable, he desired then to go from there to accomplish the rest of his plan. Coming to the mouth of the river, he dropped anchor without doing any more exploring for the rest of the day. The next day he ordered all the men to come topside because he had something to say to them. They all came up, and immediately the captain began to speak to them as follows:

"I think that all of you know that our enterprise is of great importance and greatly desired by our young king.

Therefore, my friends, desiring both your honor and your welfare, I want to explain how great an honor it will be for those of you who, with valor and true courage, will test in our first exploration the virtues and the assets of this new land. I have assured myself that this will be the greatest opportunity that you will ever have to advance yourselves in title and honor. For this reason I want to show you and set down before your eyes the eternal renown you would fully earn if, forgetting your families and your homes, you dare to undertake a thing of such importance. Even kings recognize a high degree of public service and assistance to the throne, and remember it afterwards by employing persons in serious and important enterprises, immortalizing their names forever. I ask you not to think, as many have, that such an opportunity can come to you and not be recognized by the king and the princes of the royal family. You being descended from average stock, few or none of your parents have ever made a profession of arms nor have been found among the great estates. As for myself, from my early years I applied all of my industry to follow the royal family and have hazarded my life in many dangers for the service of my king. Without this, I could never have attained this position of leadership, not that I do not deserve this title and degree of commander, but I have seen so many others receive it solely because of ancestry, being esteemed more because of their station than because of their merit. I do not overlook the fact that if we look around many can be found to deserve the title even better, and they rightly and justly should be named noble and virtuous.

"I will answer such things as you may object to concerning me personally by laying before you instead the many examples which we have from among the Romans who in point of honor were the first people to rule the world. How many among them triumphed by their own work rather than by the greatness of their parentage? If we look back among their ancestors, we find that their parents were of very low rank, survived by the common labor of their hands, and lived very poorly indeed. The father of Aelius Pertinax was a poor artisan, and his grandfather was a slave. So the histories report. Nevertheless, acting with true courage, he was not dismayed by his lowly estate but instead was ambiti-

An unidentified French leader answering to the description of Jean Ribault, a drawing from the school of François Clouet, from the collections of the Library of Congress.

ous to aspire to higher things. He began with enthusiasm to take up arms and did so well at them that, step by step, he finally became emperor of Rome. Despite all of this honor, he did not despise his parents, but instead and in memory of them he caused his father's shop to be covered with beautifully carved marble, to serve as an example to men descended from humble lineage and to give them hope to aspire to important things despite the modesty of their ancestry.

"I will not fail to mention the excellence and virtue of the valiant and redoutable Agathocles, son of a simple potter. He forgot the low estate of his father and applied himself so well in his younger years that as a result of his attainment at arms he finally became king of Sicily. In spite of this title he felt no desire to forget that he was a son of a potter. To keep alive the memory of his parents, he ordered that he be served at the table not only with vessels of gold and silver but also those of clay. He showed by this that the position he held had not been inherited but had been worked for by him alone.

"Speaking of our time, I suggest Rusten Pasha, who is well known to everybody in spite of the fact that he was the son of a poor herdsmen. He so applied his youth in virtuous living that, being brought up in the service of a great lord, he aspired to great things. And as he grew in years and increased in courage, his fine attainments acquired for him the hand of the daughter of his prince.

"These memorable examples should persuade you to stay here. Remember that for this you will always be revered as those who were the first to live in this strange land. I beg you then to discuss it among yourselves and to open your minds freely to me. I promise you to bring your names so forcefully to the ears of the king and the princes that your fame shall hereafter shine inextinguishably in the heart of France."

Scarcely had he finished his proposal when most of the soldiers responded that a greater opportunity had never come to them to render good service to their prince, agreeing also that this would increase their chances for personal recognition. They requested the captain to build them a fort before he left, and expressed hope that after a while they could finish it out. They asked him also to give them the munitions necessary for their defense. They were impatient to go forward with the project.

Jean Ribault was happy at seeing such willing men and decided the next day to look around for a place suitable and commodious enough for habitation. He embarked the next morning, telling those who were going to live there to follow him so that they would be content with the place that might be selected for settlement. Having navigated in the large river on the north side, he encountered an island which ended in a point toward the mouth of the river. Sailing a bit further, he discovered a little river which entered the interior of the island. He explored it and found it deep enough for the protection of galleys and little boats in great numbers. Proceeding farther, he found an open place upon the brink of it. He landed and, finding the place fit for the building of a fortress and agreeable to those who wanted to live there, he resolved immediately to measure out the dimensions of the fortification.[41] Considering that there were only 28 to live there,[42] he measured the fort only sixteen toises by thirteen in breadth, with flanks in proportion.[43] The measuring out was done by Captain Salles and me. We sent to the ships for men and shovels, picks, and other instruments necessary for the work and we worked so hard that in a very short time the fort was made defensible. During this time Jean Ribault had food and war munitions brought for the upkeep of the place. Having outfitted them with all they needed, he decided to go, but before leaving he talked to Captain Albert[44] whom he left as governor of the place, saying, "Captain Albert, I beg of you in the presence of everyone that you conduct yourself so wisely in your duties and so modestly govern this small group which I leave under your command and which supports your leadership in such good cheer that I shall never have occasion except to praise you and with nothing to conceal; for I am desirous to recount to the king the faithful services that you in the presence of all of us have promised to perform in this New France."

"And you, companions," he said to the soldiers, "I beg you to recognize Captain Albert as if he were myself who stayed here, giving to him the obedience which a true soldier owes to his general and captain, living as brothers one with the other without any dissension; and as you do it, God will aid and bless your work."

When he finished his speech, we took leave of them and sailed toward our ships, leaving to the fort the name Charlesfort and to the little river that of Chenonceau.[45]

Being greatly pleased at having so fortunately carried out our enterprise, we decided the next day to leave the place, hoping with luck to locate the Jordan River. We hoisted sails at ten o'clock in the morning. Then under full sail, Captain Ribault ordered a cannon salute to our French brothers in saying goodbye, and they promptly returned the salute. This done, we pushed on toward the north. And from that time on the river was named Port Royal because of its grandeur and beauty.

When we had sailed along about fifteen leagues, we saw a river and sent a barque to look it over. On their return they brought word that the mouth was only half a fathom deep. Having heard this and being rather unimpressed, we continued on our route and gave it the name of Basse River.[46] As we went on sounding each hour, we found only five or six fathoms of water even though we were a good six leagues from land. At length we found less than three fathoms. This gave us some concern, so we did not go on any farther but struck our sails, in part because of the shallowness of the water and in part because of the approaching night. During the night, Captain Jean Ribault gave thought as to whether it would be best to go on any farther in view of the obvious dangers which we saw, or if we should be content with what we had already explored, even leaving Frenchmen to occupy the land. Not being able to resolve this to his satisfaction, he put the whole thing off until the next day. Then as day came, he asked all the company what they thought best so that each would search his conscience and speak his opinion. Some said that he had reason to be content in view of the fact that he could do nothing more, reminding him that he had explored in six weeks more than the Spanish had done in two years in their New Spain, and that it would be the greatest service that could be done to the king if he would promptly return with news of his happy discoveries. Some brought up to him the depletion and damage to the foodstuffs which had occurred and the dangers which might come because of the shallow water in which they had sailed from day to day along the coast line. After careful and long debate, it was decided to leave there, turning from the northern to the eastern route which is the channel toward France. We happily arrived there on July 20, 1562.

After our departure, those at Charlesfort had no rest while, night and day, they built up their fortifications, hoping that after their fort was completed they could commence explorations up the river. One day while some of them were cutting roots in the bushes, they suddenly noticed an Indian hunting for wild animals. He was astonished at being discovered by them, but the Frenchmen went to him and spoke so humanely toward him that he was reassured and returned to Charlesfort with them. Everyone was very courteous to him there. Captain Albert was delighted at his arrival, and after having given him a shirt and some little trinkets, questioned him about his home. The Indian told him that he was from far up the river and that he was the subject of King Audusta. He indicated the boundaries of the place where he lived, doing this by hand signs. After several conversations with those at the fort, the Indian asked permission to leave because night was approaching. Captain Albert willingly gave him leave to go.

A few days afterwards, the captain decided to sail towards Audusta, and on arriving there, he was well received because of the kind of treatment that he had accorded the Indian. The king kept assuring the captain of his desire to establish friendship with him in the future, making him understand that to be an ally with him meant that there would also be four other kings as friends who in power and authority could do much for him. Moreover, in case of necessity they might help him to obtain food. One of the kings was named Mayon, another Hoya, another Touppa, and the fourth Stalame. Audusta told the captain that they would be very happy when they heard of his coming, and urged Captain Albert to visit them. The captain willingly consented, feeling that this would help to establish friendships in this area. So the next morning they departed very early and soon arrived at the house of King Touppa. Afterwards they went to the other kings' houses, except the house of King Stalame. The captain received from each of the kings all possible courtesies, and they showed themselves to be affectionate friends, offering him a thousand small presents. After he had lived among these strange kings for a few days, he took his leave and went back to the house of Audusta.

Then he gave everyone orders to re-embark because he had decided to go to the home of Stalame, whose place was fifteen leagues north of Charlesfort. Sailing then in the full current of the river, they reached the home of Stalame, who took all the men in and gave them the best of the food that he had. He presented Captain Albert with his bow and arrows, doing this as a sign of alliance between them. He also gave him some chamois skin. The captain, on observing that most of the day had passed, took leave of King Stalame to return to Charlesfort, and he arrived there the next day.

The friendship was so great between our people and King Audusta that almost everything was shared in common, and this Indian king did not do anything unusual without advising us of it. So as the time approached for the celebration of the feast of Toya, strange ceremonies to tell about, he sent ambassadors to the French to invite them to take part and assist. This they willingly accepted because they wanted to know about this ceremony, and they embarked and navigated to the home of the king who had already graciously come forward to greet them. After expressing his good will, he conducted them to his house and made it a point to treat them as well as he knew how.

All of the Indians prepared to celebrate the feast the next day. The king took the Frenchmen to see the place where the feast would be held. There they saw women working in every way to make the area clean and neat. This place was in the form of a large circle of earth with an open prospect. The next morning all those who were to take part in the celebration were painted and plumed in many different colors, and went from the king's house toward the place of Toya. Arriving there they arranged themselves in order and followed three Indians who were painted in a way to make them look different from the others. Everyone carried a small drum in his hand. Then they began to enter the middle of the circle, dancing and singing in doleful tones, followed by others who answered them. After they had sung, danced, and turned three times, they ran like unbridled horses into the midst of the thickest woods; and the women continued throughout the rest of the day crying as sadly as possible. Then they grabbed the arms of young girls in a fury, and cut them so cruelly with sharp clam shells that the blood flowed. Then they sprang into the air crying "He Toya" three times.

King Audusta brought all our Frenchmen into his house for the feast. He was provoked at their laughter and arranged for them to be inside, because Indians are very sensitive about being seen in their religious ceremonies. Nevertheless, one of our Frenchmen cleverly removed himself from Audusta's house and hid himself behind a big bush where at his pleasure he could easily watch the ceremonies of the feast. The three who began the feast ceremonies were called "joanas," and they were priests or executioners of the Indian law and were given faith and confidence in part because of an inherited right to order sacrificial ceremonies and in part because they are clever magicians who can quickly recover lost objects. Yet they are revered, not just because of these things, but mostly because they heal diseases through their knowledge of herbs.

Those who had run into the woods returned two days afterwards. Upon returning, they began to dance in the center of the place and by their gaiety and enthusiasm cheered up their good Indian fathers who because of age or because of natural feebleness had not entered into the festival. When all the dances were ended, they began to eat with such greediness that they seemed to devour their meat rather than eat it, for they had neither eaten nor drunk anything during the day of the festival nor in the two days following. Our Frenchmen were not forgotten in this good cheer, for the Indians sent for them, saying that they were very happy to have them there.

One of our Frenchmen having lived for some time with the Indians, gained acquaintanceship with a young lad and asked him what the Indians did when they were absent in the woods. The youth made him understand by signs that the joanas had prayed to Toya and that by magic signs they had made him come to them so that they might speak to him and demand very strange things of him, which for fear of the joanas he dared not describe. There are also several other ceremonies which I will not recount here, lest I bore my readers with inconsequential things.

When the feast was finished, our Frenchmen returned to Charlesfort. After they had been there for a short time, the food began to run short. This forced them to go to their neighbors for assistance in their necessities. The neighbors gave them part of everything they had, except the seed grain they needed for sowing their fields. They told the Frenchmen further that because of this they would have to go into the woods themselves to live on acorns and roots until the time of harvest should come. Being very sorry that they were not able to give any further aid, they advised the Frenchmen to go to the country of King Covecxis, a man of might and renown who lived in the southern part of this land, where there was an abundance in all seasons and a great supply of corn, flour, and beans. They said that by his sole assistance they could live a very long time, but that before going to that land it would be wise to get permission from a king named Oade, a brother of Covecxis, who in corn, flour, and beans was no less rich or generous and who would be glad to see them.[47]

Our Frenchmen, having heard the good reputation these Indians gave those two kings, decided to go there because they felt that the urgency had already arisen. They then asked King Maccou if he would let them have one of his subjects to guide them on the right path. He was glad to do this service because he knew that without this they could hardly carry out their plan.

When they had placed everything in order for the trip, they put to sea and navigated to the land of Oade, which they found on the Belle River.[48] On their arrival they saw a band of Indians, who quickly came out to meet them. As the Indians came forward, their guards made a sign that Oade was in this band, whereupon our Frenchmen advanced to salute him. Then two of his sons who accompanied him, handsome and powerful men, saluted in a friendly manner and showed themselves to be amiable.

The king promptly made an oration in his Indian language, expressing great pleasure in seeing them in his place and saying that he would be their true ally against those who would wish to be enemies. After his speech he led them to this house where he made an effort to entertain them graciously. His house was decorated with tapestries of various colored feathers up to the height of a pike. The place where the king slept was covered with white coverlets embroidered with fine workmanship and fringed in scarlet. There the king was advised by one of the guides as to why they had taken to the sea and had come there. The Frenchmen said that, having heard of his generosity, they sought help with food, which was their great need and necessity, and that in return they would be faithful and loyal friends and defenders against all of his enemies in the future. This good Indian was as ready to do the favor as they were to ask it and he commanded his subjects to fill our boat with corn and beans. Then he had six pieces of tapestry brought out, made like little blankets, and presented them to the French in such generosity that he easily proved to the French that he desired to be friendly. In reciprocation for all these gifts, the Frenchmen presented him with two sickles and some other merchandise. This seemed to fully satisfy him. As the Frenchmen took their leave, the king urged their prompt return and assured them that if their food ran short it would never be his fault as long as he was in power. The Frenchmen then embarked and sailed toward Charlesfort, perhaps 25 leagues away.

Just as our Frenchmen thought that they could take things a little easier and be free from the dangers to which they had been exposed night and day, getting together food here and there, then as they slept fire caught up their lodgings with such a fury, increased by the wind, that the great room that was built for them before our departure was consumed in an instant. Nothing was saved except a small amount of food.

For this reason our Frenchmen were at the end of their rope, in a totally helpless situation except for the mercy of God. God, who knows the hearts and minds of men, never forsakes those who need Him. So early the next morning King Audusta and King Maccou came accompanied by a large number of Indians, and recognizing the misfortune, they were greatly concerned and proposed that all of their subjects speedily build another house, avowing that the French were their esteemed friends and that proof of this had already been given by the presents which they had received. They said that anyone who did not put his full power into helping would be considered as useless and as having no good in him at all, a judgment which these people believe to be worse than any other. So each one began to exert himself, and in less than twelve hours they built a house quite perfectly, and no smaller than the first one. Having completed it, they returned home very pleased with a few sickles and axes which they had accepted from our men.

Within a short time after this misfortune, the food supply began to run out again, and after our Frenchmen had deliberated, thinking and rethinking, they decided the best thing to do was to return to King Oade and to King Covecxis, his brother. They resolved to send there a few of their men on the following day. They traveled in an Indian small boat[49] by the inland passage[50] for about ten leagues and found a large and good fresh-water river, which they reconnoitered. They observed many crocodiles which surpassed in size those of the Nile River. The shores were lined with great cypress trees. After staying for a while, they pushed on, being well assisted by the tides and without being subjected to the hazards of the sea. In this way they arrived at Oade's place, where they were well received. They told him why they had returned to see him and of the unfortunate accident which had happened since their last trip. They advised him that the fire had destroyed not only their household stuffs but also the food which he had given them so bountifully, and that for this reason they had come to him again to ask aid in their necessities. When the king understood, he sent an ambassador to his brother Covecxis, requesting him to send corn and beans. This he did and very early the next morning they came back with the foodstuffs, which the king had ordered placed in their small boat.

Our Frenchmen were very pleased at this generosity and asked leave to depart. For the day he would not allow it and attempted to give them as much happiness as he could before they left. The next day in the morning he took them to see the place where the corn grew and told them that they should not be in want as long as the corn lasted. Then he gave them a number of excellent pearls and two fine crystal stones and some silver ore. In return for these gifts our Frenchmen gave him some small things and inquired as to the place from which the silver and crystal had come. He replied that it was a ten-day journey away from his house and in the interior; and that the people there dug this out of the foot of certain high mountains where they found it in large quantities. Happy to learn such good news and having found out more than they had set out to discover, they took leave of the king and returned by the same route by which they had come.

Our Frenchmen conducted themselves very well up to this time, despite their misfortunes. But misfortune, or more accurately, the judgment of God, decreed that those who could not even be overcome by fire and water could nevertheless destroy themselves. It is common among men that they cannot tolerate living without change, and would rather ruin themselves than be deprived of something new every day. There are plenty of examples in ancient history, principally among the Romans. This little group of men far away from their homeland and abandoned by their fellow citizens can be added to the list.

They entered then into partialities and dissensions, having for their beginning cause the treatment of a soldier named Guernache, a drummer who was very popular among his French companions. According to what was told me, he was very cruelly treated by his captain and for a rather minor offense. This captain continued to threaten the French soldiers in order to make them obey. They would not obey him as they should have done; and this caused a mutiny, because many times he put his threats of punishment into execution. They kept after him to such an extent that finally they put him to death. The principal occasion for this was his downgrading of a soldier named Lachère, whom he had banished, and his failing to keep his promise to send him food every eight days. He said that on the contrary he would be glad to hear of his death. Moreover, he promised that he would chastize others among them, and he used such rough language that good taste prevents me from repeating it.

The soldiers, observing that his unreasonableness increased from day to day and fearing that they might fall into the same dangers as Lachère, decided to kill the captain. Having done this, they brought back the banished soldier, who had been on a small island about three leagues from Charlesfort. They found him about half dead from hunger.

On returning, they all assembled to elect a new governor among them, and they named Captain Nicolas Barré, a man worthy of command.[51] He knew so well how to carry out his responsibilities that rancor and dissension ended among them and they lived peacefully among themselves.

Notwithstanding this, they commenced to build a little boat, hoping to go back to France if no help came to them such as they had been expecting from day to day. There was not a man among them who knew the art of boat-building. Still, necessity teaches everything and showed them the way. After building it, they gave thought to equipping it with everything that would be necessary for their journey. However the things they needed most, like cords and sails, were lacking. Having no means to procure these things, they were more depressed than before and fell into a miserable despair.

But God never forsakes those in need, and helped them in their necessity. While they were in the midst of their perplexities, King Audusta and King Maccou came with at least two hundred Indians; and our Frenchmen went out to meet them and told the kings about the necessity of having ropes. The kings promised to return within two days and to bring them a quantity sufficient to equip the boat. Happy with this good news and with the promises, they gave the Indians a number of sickles and shirts. After they left, our Frenchmen sought by every possible means to get resin in the woods. They cut the bark of the pines and brought out enough to cover the boat. Also to caulk the boat they gathered a kind of moss which grows on trees in this area. They now lacked nothing but the sails, and these they made from their shirts and bedclothes. Several days afterward, the Indians returned to Charlesfort with many ropes, which were found ample to equip the small boat.[52]

Our men were now as happy as could be. They were generous toward the Indians in leaving the country and gave them all the merchandise that remained. By this means they left the Indians fully satisfied as they departed. Our Frenchmen continued to perfect the ship and worked so diligently that in a little time it was ready in everything.

Then the wind picked up and seemed to invite them to put to sea. This they did after putting everything in final order; but before leaving, they put on board the artillery, the forge, and other munitions that Captain Ribault had left with them. It took up more room than they had provided for the corn. Being carried away by the excessive joy which they felt in returning to France, not being thoughtful and not considering the unreliability of the wind, which changes in a moment, they put to sea with such meager rations that the enterprise became a sad and desperate one.

After they had navigated their course about a third of the way, they were depressed at the calms which came and because in three weeks they had not advanced more than 25 leagues. During this time the food diminished and became so short in supply that they were required to eat no more than twelve grains of corn a day, this being in food value about as much as twelve peas. Yet even this ration did not continue long, for all at once all food was gone and they had no other recourse than to eat their shoes and leather jackets. This they did. As for drink, some used sea water, others their urine. They remained in such desperate need for such a long time that some of them died from hunger. Besides the extreme famine which oppressed them, each minute of every hour they lost more hope of seeing France again. They were forced continually to bail out the boat because water entered on all sides, and every day things were worse and worse. After they had eaten their shoes and leather jerkins, a tremendous wind came up and it was so contrary to their course that in no time at all the boat was half filled with water and broken in on one side.

It now seemed almost hopeless to escape from their extreme peril, and they gave up on bailing out the water. It was about to drown them. They fell over backward as men ready to die and gave their souls over to the will of the waves. But one among them still had spirit and told them they only had a short distance to go, assuring them that if the wind held out they would see land within three days. This man encouraged them so much that they bailed out the boat again and remained three days without eating or drinking except for sea water.

When the time of his promise had expired, they were in more grief than before because they did not see any land. So, in this last despair, some of them proposed that it would be better that one die than that all should perish. They agreed that one should die to sustain the others. The one who was executed was Lachère. His flesh was equally divided among his companions, a thing so pitiful to recite that my pen is loath to write about it.

After this long and perilous journey, God in His goodness changed their sorrow into joy and showed them the land. They were so ecstatic about it that they remained for a time as men without sense, letting the boat drift this way and that. But a little English rowboat came up to their boat, and in the rowboat was a Frenchman who had been on a previous voyage to New France, and he easily understood and talked with them. The Englishmen gave food and drink to our Frenchmen, who quickly recovered their courage and told them about their trip. The English consulted a long time about what they should do with our Frenchmen, and finally decided to put the sick ones on land and to take the others to the queen of England, who at the time was planning an expedition into New France.[53] Briefly, that is what happened to those whom Captain Jean Ribault left in New France.

Now I shall continue my account. After arrival at Dieppe, which was on July 20, 1562, we found that civil wars had begun. This was partly the reason why our men had not been relieved as Captain Jean Ribault had promised them. And from this it followed that Captain Albert was killed by his own men and the land abandoned, as I have discussed before and as one can learn in more detail from those who were actually present.

The Second Voyage of the French to Florida, Made by Captain Laudonnière in 1564

AFTER PEACE was declared in France, the Admiral of Châtillon remonstrated with the king that there had been no news of the men whom Captain Jean Ribault had left in Florida and that it would be a great pity to lose them.[54] Because of this, the king gave him permission to equip three ships, one of 120 tons, another of 100 tons, and a third of 60 tons, to seek them out and give them aid.[55]

The admiral, then being well informed of the faithful service that I had rendered to His Majesty as well as his predecessor kings of France, advised the king how able I was to serve him on this expedition. This was the reason why he made me commander of these three ships and told me to depart promptly

Charles IX, aged eighteen in 1568, an engraving from the collections of the Library of Congress.

to perform his orders. Not desiring to do otherwise and feeling very happy at being selected from a large number of others who were very able to acquit themselves in this responsibility, I embarked at Havre de Grâce on April 22, 1564, and assembled my vessels as we approached the coast of England.

Then I turned toward the south to sail directly to the Fortunate Islands, presently called the Canaries, one of which is called the Deserted Island because it has no inhabitants. It was the first that our ships passed. Sailing forward, we landed the next day at Tenerife. This is also called the Pike because in its midst there is a very high mountain, nearly as high as Aetna, which rises up like a pike. No man can go up on the top of it except from the middle of May to the middle of August because of the great cold which is there during the entire year. This is unusual considering that it is not more than 27½° from the equator. We saw it all covered with snow, although it was by then the fifth of May.

The natives of this island, when attacked by the Spanish, withdrew to this mountain.[56] There for a space of time they fought, not willing to give up their independence nor to lose their island either by force or by alliance. Of those who had gone to live with the Spaniards not a single man returned to tell of it. Finally all of the natives who had lived there died because they could not survive in this cold place so foreign to their nature and because they lacked there the things necessary for their livelihood.

After refreshing myself with the sweet fresh water that came from a spring at the bottom of the mountain, I continued my course toward the west, where the winds favored me so well that fifteen days later our ships arrived safe and sound at the Antilles. I went on shore at the Isle of Martinique, one of the first of them. The next day we arrived at Dominica, twelve leagues farther on than the first.

Dominica is one of the most beautiful of the western islands, mountainous and of sweet-smelling air. In passing through, we desired to see the sights that were there and also to replace our supply of fresh water; so I dropped anchor along the coast. As soon as this happened, two Indians came to us in two little boats full of excellent fruit called ananas [pineapples]. As they approached our barque, one of them was in doubt about us and returned to land, running away. Our men, perceiving this, caught the poor Indian in the other little boat, and he was so astonished at seeing us that he did not know how to behave. I understood afterwards that he had feared that he had fallen into the hands of Spaniards. These had once captured him and had cut out his testicles, as he showed us. This poor Indian was reassured after a time, and we discussed several things with him, doing this awkwardly because we understood nothing except through the signs that he thought up. Finally he asked leave to depart and promised me a thousand presents. I agreed provided that he would have patience to wait until the next day when we would set foot on the island. When we landed I let him go, after I had given him a shirt and certain trifles. This made him happy as he left us.

The place where we went on shore was near a very high rock, and from it flowed a little river of excellent fresh water. We stayed by this river several days and reconnoitered the things that seemed worth visiting.

Portrait of Catherine de Medici by François Clouet, from a photograph of the same in the collections of the Library of Congress.

We traded a little with the Indians, and they begged us not to go near their homes or their gardens. They said to do so would give them great displeasure, and they promised that we would have no shortage of pineapples. These we purchased with some inexpensive merchandise. One day some of our Frenchmen, who were anxious to see something new in this strange land, followed the path through the woods and arrived at the bank of a little river. Following the bank of this river, they noticed two great snakes which were in their way. My soldiers went ahead of the snakes, trying to keep them from entering the woods, but the serpents were not frightened and glided into the bushes, hissing loudly. Swords in hand, my men attacked them and later found that the snakes were nine feet long and as thick as a man's leg.

After this encounter some of the less discreet of my men gathered pineapples from Indian gardens, carelessly going into the very middle of them. With even less discretion they went toward the homes of the Indians. This made the Indians so angry that they rushed out furiously, let their arrows fly, and hit one of my men, named Martin Chauveau. He remained behind and we never knew whether he was killed on the spot or made a prisoner. Those of his company who were with him had enough of the affair, and each saved himself without worrying about companions. When M. d'Ottigni, my lieutenant, learned of this, he sent word to me to ask whether I thought it would be a good idea to lay an ambush for the Indians who had taken or killed the man, or whether he should go directly to their houses to learn the truth. After thinking it over, I sent him word not to do anything about these events but to embark promptly with all those who were on the island. This he did immediately. But as he navigated toward the ships, he saw along the shoreline a large number of Indians, all shooting their arrows. For his part he discharged his guns against them, but he was unable to hurt them or even to alarm them. So he gave up and came back to the ship, where we remained until the next morning.

Then we set sail in the charted route and navigated among the isles conquered by the Spanish, such as St. Christopher, Iles des Saintes, Montserrat, and Redonda. Then we passed between Anguillo and Anegada, continuing toward New France.

We arrived at New France fifteen days afterwards, on Thursday, June 22, at about three or four o'clock in the afternoon. We landed near a little river which is 30 degrees distant from the equator and ten leagues above Cape François, measuring from the south; and about thirty leagues from the River of May. After we struck sails and cast anchor athwart the river, I determined to go ashore and reconnoiter, since three or four hours of afternoon were available. I went accompanied by M. d'Ottigni and M. d'Arlac, my ensign, and a considerable number of gentlemen and soldiers. I sounded the channel at the mouth and found it to be very shallow, although further on it was reasonably deep. The river separates itself into two great arms, one running south and the other north.

Having reconnoitered the river, I landed to talk to the Indians who waited for us on the bank. They cried out with a loud voice in their native language "Antipola bonnassou," which means "brother," "friend," or something like that. After they had made much of us, they introduced their paraousti, or king or chief, to whom I presented certain trinkets. This pleased him immensely. For my part, I praised God without ceasing for the great affection that I found among these savages. They were unhappy at nothing except that the night approached which would take us away. Though they endeavored by every means to make us trade with them and explained by signs that they wanted to give us some presents, nevertheless for various good reasons I decided not to stay. Excusing myself from all their offered presents, I re-embarked and went toward my ships. However, before leaving, I named this river the River of Dolphins, because on my arrival I had seen a large number of dolphins playing about in the mouth of the river.[57]

Since toward the south I had not found a suitable place in which to live and build a fort, on the next day, the twenty-third of the month, I gave orders to lift anchors, let out sails, and navigate toward the River of May. We arrived there two days afterwards and cast anchor. Then having landed with quite a number of gentlemen and soldiers to explore the place, we saw the chief of that country, who came to meet us. It was the same one whom we had seen on the voyage under Captain Jean Ribault. Having seen us he cried out from the distance, "Antipola, antipola," and showed such enthusiasm that he almost lost his composure. He came up to us, accompanied by two of his children, as handsome and as powerful as any that you can find on earth, who offered us only friendship by repeating the word "friend, friend." Recognizing some of us from the preceding voyage, they addressed themselves chiefly to these in using words of friendship. There were many in the gathering, both men and women, who made much of us and by signs showed their happiness that we had come.

Then the chief suggested going to see the stone column that we had erected during the voyage of Jean Ribault, and of which I have already spoken. It was a thing to which they ascribed great significance. Having granted their request to go to the place where the stone was set up, we found it to be crowned with magnolia garlands and at its foot there were little baskets of corn which they called in their language "tapaga tapola." They kissed the stone on their arrival with great reverence and asked us to do the same. As a matter of friendship we could not refuse, and when this was done the chief took me by the hand as if he had a great secret to tell me, and showed me by signs how far up the river his dominion lay. He said that he was called Paracousi Satouriona, which amounts to King Satouriona. The children carry the same title of paraousti. His oldest one is named Atore, a man whom I dare say is perfect in handsomeness, wisdom, and honest appearance, showing by his modest dignity that he earned the title that he carried. Also, he was pleasant and easy to associate with. After I had spent a little time with them, the chief asked one of his sons to present a slab of silver to me, which he did willingly. As a reward, I gave a knife and some other more expensive presents with which he seemed to be very well pleased. Then, as night approached, we took our leave and returned to go to bed on board ship.

Being delighted by this good treatment, I returned the next day with my lieutenant and a number of soldiers to visit the chief of the River of May. He waited for us at the same place where we had talked to him the day before. We found him in the shade of an arbor, accompanied by eighty Indians. He was clothed in a great deerskin, dressed out like chamois and painted in strange designs of various colors. The paintings were so naturally charming and still so consistent with the rules of art that no professional artist could find fault with them. The natural ability of these strange people is so perfectly adjusted that, without sophisticated artistry, they can content the eye of the trained artist, even the perfectionist.

I advised Chief Satouriona that I wished to explore up the river, but that we would return promptly and that I would come again to him in a short time. He said that this was all right and that he would stay in the place where he was. As a token of his promise he presented me with the beautiful deerskin. I refused it and told him that I would take it on my return. I gave him a number of little trinkets to keep our friendship alive.

I had not sailed more than three leagues up the river, being always followed by the Indians alongside crying, "friend, friend," when I discovered a mountain of modest height. I landed at the foot of this and there met some men who were working with corn. In a corner of the field there was a house built for the persons who guarded the corn. So many birds live in this land and continually attack the corn that the Indians have to guard it, for otherwise they would lose their entire harvest. I stayed there for several hours and sent M. d'Ottigni and my sergeant into the woods to observe the dwelling places of the Indians.

After they had been on the path for a while, they came to a marsh of reeds where the path came to an end. They rested under the shade of a large magnolia tree and considered what they should do next. Then they discovered five Indians half covered in the woods. They seemed to be afraid of the Frenchmen until our men said to them the Indian words, "Antipola bonnassou." When they heard this they came right out. Since the four who came last lifted the deerskin of the first, our Frenchmen believed that the first was a man of higher station than the others, so they called him chief. Some of our company went toward him and indicated their friendship and pointed out M. d'Ottigni, the lieutenant, for whom they had made an arbor of magnolia and palm in the Indian fashion so that the savages would know by these acts that our Frenchmen had associations with such as they in previous times.

The Indian chief came up to our Frenchmen and made a long speech which really had no other purpose than to invite them to come to his home to see his parents, which our Frenchmen agreed to do. As a token of his good will, he gave Lieutenant Ottigni the skin that he was wearing. Then taking him by the hand, he led Ottigni along the marshes. The chief and M. Ottigni and certain others of our Frenchmen were carried over the marshes on the backs of Indians. Others, who could not get across because of the mire and reeds, went through the woods and followed a narrow path which went right to the chief's dwelling. From this building about fifty Indians came out to welcome our Frenchmen and to feast them according to their means. After that they brought in a great clay bowl which was curiously made and full of excellent, clear spring water. This bowl was carried by an Indian and there was another young Indian who carried this same kind of water in a little vessel of wood. He presented it for drinking to each one in turn, following a certain order of rank among them as they were invited to drink.

Thirst being quenched in this way and our Frenchmen being refreshed, the chief took them to the lodgings of his father, one of the oldest persons on earth. Our Frenchmen, respecting his extreme old age, commenced by calling out, "Friend, friend"; and the old man responded pleasantly. Then they interrogated him about his age, and he answered that he was the oldest in a line of five generations, and he showed them another old man who sat across from him and who far exceeded him in age. This was his father and he resembled a dead carcass more than a living man. His sinews, veins, arteries, bones, and other parts appeared through his skin in such a way that they all stood out from each other. He was so old that he had lost his sight and could speak only one word at a time and even that with exceeding difficulty.

M. d'Ottigni, having seen this strange spectacle, spoke to the younger of the two old men and asked him further about his age. Then the old man called in a group of Indians and, striking twice upon his thigh and laying his hand upon two of them, he showed him by signs that these two were his sons. Then striking their thighs, he showed him others not so old who were the children of those first two, which procedure continued in the same manner until the fifth generation. Yet this old man had a father still alive, older of course than himself. Both of them wore their pure white hair long. It had been told them that they might yet live thirty or forty more years in the course of nature, even though the younger of them was not less than 250 years old.

After he had finished talking, he gave an order that our Frenchmen be given two young eagles which were pets in his house. Also he gave our Frenchmen little palm baskets full of red and blue gourds. In return for these gifts he was satisfied with some French trinkets. The two old men ordered that our party be guided back again to the place from which they came, by the same young chief who had brought them to the house. The Frenchmen then came back to the place where I had stopped and told me what they had seen, asking me to reward their guide who had so good-naturedly received them in his home. This I did.

Now I was determined to investigate the mount, and I went right to the top, which we found covered by cedar, palm, and magnolia trees.[58] These gave a fragrance so delightful that perfume could not improve upon it. The trees were all entwined with cords of vines, bearing grapes in such quantities that their number would be sufficient to render the place habitable. Besides this fertility as a vineyard, one could see large quantities of chinaroot growing around in the bushes. Concerning the pleasantness of the place, the sea may be seen clearly and openly from it, and more than six leagues off toward the Belle River one may see broad meadows divided by isles and islets interlacing each other.[59] Briefly, the place is so pleasant that it would force the depressed to lift their spirits.

The Second Voyage 65

After I stayed there for a while, I re-embarked with my men to navigate toward the mouth of the river. There we found the chief, true to his promise, waiting for us. In order to keep him happy, we landed and paid him the homage required of us. Then he gave me the richly painted skin which he carried, and I returned the favor with an assortment of our merchandise. I asked him where he got the slab of silver which he had given me. To this he made a quick response which I could not comprehend. He noticed that I could not understand and showed me by signs that it came from a place far up the river and several days distant from the river, and that all they had of it they took by force of arms from the people of that place called by them "Thimogona."[60] He strongly asserted that these were their most ancient and natural enemies.

Having noticed that he spoke rather emotionally when he pronounced the word "Thimogona," I understood what he wanted me to say. To increase his friendship I promised to go with all my forces to assist him in battle there. This made him so happy that from then on he promised victory, and he assured me that within a short time he would make a voyage to that place after he had prepared food in a sufficient quantity and instructed his men to fix their bows and to furnish themselves adequately with arrows so that nothing would be lacking for combat against the Thimogona. He begged me finally and very affectionately not to back down on my promise, and he expressed the hope of seizing gold and silver in large quantities so that my desires would be met along with his.

All of this being decided, I took my leave and returned to the ships. There we rested ourselves for the following night, and very early the next day we hoisted sails and navigated toward the Seine River, about four leagues distant from the River of May. Continuing our route to the north, we arrived at the mouth of the Somme River, which is not more than six leagues from the Seine River. There we dropped anchor and landed so that we could explore the place just as we had done at other locations.

Here we were graciously and pleasantly received by the chief of the area, who was one of the tallest and best proportioned men that I have ever seen. His wife sat by his side. Over and above her Indian beauty, with which she was greatly endowed, she had such a virtuous countenance and modest gravity that there was not one among us who did not greatly praise her. At her side were five of her daughters. All of these were well formed, and so polite that I easily concluded that their mother had been their teacher and had shown them what was right and how to develop their character. After the chief had received us, as I have mentioned, he told his wife to present me with a number of little balls of silver, and for his own part he presented me with his bow and arrows as he had done with Captain Jean Ribault on our first voyage, this for a sign of perpetual friendship and alliance.

In discussion of one thing and another, the subject of weapons came up. Then the chief had a target erected to test our guns against his arrows. But that did not work out well for him because as soon as he knew that our guns could pierce easily what his arrows could not even scratch, it vexed him greatly to understand how that could be so. In the meantime, wishing to conceal in his thoughts what his face openly disclosed, he changed the subject and begged us to spend the night at his house, saying that a grander hour would never come to his household and that he wanted to repay us with a thousand presents.

Nevertheless, we could not grant him this point and took leave of him to return to our ships. There, shortly afterwards, I caused all of my company to be assembled with the masters and pilots for a consultation on where we should plant our home. First I mentioned what they all knew, that the tip of Florida was a marshy area and therefore unsuitable for our habitation, as it was a place which would bring neither profit to the king nor contentment or pleasure to us if we inhabited that land. On the other hand, if we went northward to look over Port Royal, we would not find it very comfortable or usable, at least if we were to believe the reports of those who had lived there for a long time. Although the harbor there was one of the finest in the West Indies, the issue was not so much a question of the beauty of the location but more a question of the availability of things necessary to sustain daily life. In our first year it would be much more important to live in a place with an abundant food supply than to be in a commodious and beautiful port, even if it were very deep and very pleasant to see. I was of the opinion, and it seemed good to them, that we should set ourselves up around the River of May, since on our first voyage we had found it to abound in corn and material for flour, to say nothing of the gold and silver that was found there, a thing which gave me hope for some future happy discovery.

After I had stated these things, each one expressed his opinion and all finally resolved, particularly those who had been with me in the first voyage, that it was better to become established on the River of May than on any other river, until we might hear news from France. This point being agreed upon, we turned the bows of our ships toward that river and with diligence and lucky winds we arrived the next morning about dawn, which was Thursday, the twenty-ninth of the month.[61] Anchors were dropped and I had all our furniture and the soldiers loaded in small boats to sail toward the mouth of the river. Entering it and at some distance upstream, we found a creek of substantial size, which invited us to refresh ourselves a little as we rested; and then we landed to look over a place which was free of trees and which we had observed from the creek. We decided that this locality was not ideal for habitation; and so we determined to return to the location that we had first discovered when we were navigating the river. This place, next to the mountain, seemed better and more convenient for the building of a fortress than where we were at the time of our decision.

We walked there through the forests and were guided by the young chief who had taken us to his father. We found a spacious countryside with high pine trees growing close together, and under these we noticed a large number of deer gamboling across the open spaces through which we passed. Then we found a hillside on the edge of a great green valley, and in its open spaces there were the most beautiful prairies in all the world, and the grass was of a good type for pasture. It was surrounded by little fresh-water streams and by a tall forest which made the valley very beautiful to see. After consideration I agreed to name it, on the request of my soldiers, the Vale of Laudonnière.[62]

We pushed forward. Then on a little trail we encountered an Indian of tall stature, who was an hermaphrodite. She brought us a large vessel full of fresh spring water. This greatly refreshed us because we were much weakened by the broiling heat which beat down through those high forests. I think that without the help of that Indian, or more without the great desire we had to carry out our resolution, we would have stayed all night in the woods. Being refreshed in this manner, we picked up our spirits, vigorously pushed ahead, and arrived at the place we had decided upon as our home. In no time at all we had fixed up some boughs of trees on the edge of the river as beds for the coming night. These we found very restful because of the work that we had done in the preceding day and in all our marching about.

The next morning at daybreak[63] I ordered a trumpet to sound so that we could assemble and give thanks to God for our favorable and happy arrival. We sang songs of thanksgiving to God and prayed that it would please Him of His holy grace to continue His accustomed goodness toward us, His poor servants, and to give us aid in all our enterprises so that all might redound to His great glory and to the advancement of our king. The prayers being ended, everyone began to take courage.

Then, having measured out a piece of ground in the form of a triangle, we went to work, some to dig on all sides, others to cut fagots, and others to raise and give form to the rampart. There was not a man among us who did not have either a shovel, a cutting

Laudonnière.

Portrait of René Laudonnière with coat of arms, reproduced from Léon Guérin, Les Navigateurs français (*Paris, Bertrand, 1847*).

hook, or a hatchet, either for clearing out the trees or for building the fort. We worked with such enthusiasm that within a few days the effect of our work was apparent. During this time Chief Satouriona, our nearest neighbor and on whose ground we built our fort, visited us, usually accompanied by his two sons and by a number of Indians, offering to be of service. For my part, I gave him various articles of merchandise so that he would know the good will we bore to him and so that he would be anxious for our friendship. As the days went on, our friendship and alliance increased in strength.

Our fort having been completed, I began to build a barn for the storage of supplies and the things that were necessary for the defense of the fort. I asked the chief to tell his subjects to make a roof of palmetto leaves—because that is the only cover they put over buildings there—so that in succeeding days I might unload our ships and put under cover those things that were still on board. The chief promptly commanded, in my presence, that all Indians in his company should gather palmetto leaves; and so the barn was covered in two days. During this time the Indians worked hard, some bringing palmetto leaves and others weaving them together. In this way the order of their chief was carried out just as he wished it.

Our fort was built in a triangle. The side to the west, the land side, was enclosed by a little moat under turfs turned up into the form of a parapet about nine feet high. The other side, which was toward the river, was enclosed with a palisade of planks of timber in the manner in which dikes are made. It had on the south side a form of bastion where I had a barn built for munitions. All of it was constructed of fagots and earth except for two or three feet of turf from which the parapets were made. I made a great place in the middle about eighteen paces long and wide and had a guardhouse built in the center of this on the south side and a residence building on the other side toward the north. We made this a little too high because shortly afterwards the wind blew it down, and experience taught me that it was not wise to build to a great height in that land because of the fierce winds to which it is subject.

One of the sides which formed my court, which I had made good and spacious, was bounded by the munitions storehouse; and on the other side toward the river was my house, around which were covered galleries. The principal door of my quarters was in the middle of the court, and the other door was toward the river. I had an oven built at some distance from the fort because the houses were covered with palmetto leaves and when fire starts in them it is hard to put out. There, in brief, is a description of our fortress, which I named "la Caroline" in honor of King Charles.

After we had done the most necessary things, I did not want to let a minute pass without putting it to some good use. Therefore I charged M. d'Ottigni, my lieutenant and an honest and able man, to reconnoiter up the river among the Thimogona, of whom Chief Satouriona had spoken so often on our coming to shore. The chief furnished two Indian guides to aid him, and they were so anxious to fight with their enemies that they seemed as happy as if they were going to a wedding.

Having embarked and raised sails, they proceeded about twenty leagues, with the Indians always on the lookout for enemies. The Indians finally spied three little boats and quickly called out "Thimogona, Thimogona," and would speak of nothing else but going into battle right away. This the captain feigned to agree to do in order to quiet them down. When they came closer, one of the Indians seized a halberd and the other a cutlass and they appeared to want to jump right into the water to go fight their enemies.

D'Ottigni would not let them do it; and, instead of closing in on the other Indians, allowed them to turn the prows of their little boats toward the shore so that they could escape into the woods. The plan of d'Ottigni was not to make war on the Thimogona but rather to make friends and, if possible, to make all the Indians live in peace with each other, hoping by this to forward our discoveries, particularly as to the true course of the river. With this purpose in mind he ordered the barque which had the two Indian guides in it to hold back and he went forward with his men toward the little boats which were on the river bank. Having come to the boats, he put a few trifles in them and then pulled away. This brought the Indians back and let them know that those in our barque were not enemies, but instead had come to trade with them. Being thus assured of our intentions, they called to our men to come closer. This they did promptly and upon landing our men spoke freely with the Indians, doing this with the usual ceremonies which are too long to recount here.

Finally d'Ottigni asked them by signs if they had any gold or silver with them. They told him that they did not have any just then, but that if he could send one of his men with them, they would lead him safely to a place where they could obtain it. D'Ottigni, finding that they were so willing and friendly, designated one of his men who seemed to want to take the trip. This soldier stayed with them until ten o'clock the following morning. Captain d'Ottigni in the meantime, somewhat put out by this long delay, navigated ten leagues farther up the river, although he did not know the exact course to take. As he went on, he encountered a little boat with his soldier in it. The soldier reported that the Indians had expected him to take a three-day journey from there and had told him that Mayrra, the king they were to visit, was rich in gold and silver and that for a small amount of merchandise one could buy substantial amounts of metal from him. Yet the soldier said that he would not take this journey without permission. He observed that so far he had not brought back very much gold. So the matter was settled with our men returning to the fort of la Caroline and leaving the soldier with the Indians so that he could look into things more at his leisure.

Fifteen days after this trip to the Thimogona, I sent Captain Vasseur and also my sergeant again into this country to inquire about the soldier who had remained behind from the former trip there. After embarking, they navigated two entire days. Before they arrived at the dwelling place of the Indians, they found two Indians on the river bank who were there as lookouts for any enemy who might come into their area for a surprise attack, the usual method of attack.

When they saw Captain Vasseur, they realized that he was not one of their enemies, so it was not difficult for our men to approach them in the barque. They made known by signs that the soldier who was sought was not there but presently was at the home of King Molona, a vassal of another great king, identified by them as Olata Ouae Outina. They said that if the captain wished to go to that place, he could be there quickly. He agreed to this and set out for the place that the Indians had indicated. This made them so happy that they ran ahead along the land route to announce his coming. Vasseur reached the residence of King Molona after being rowed for only about half a league. Soon after King Molona had received Captain Vasseur and his men, our soldier came in, carrying five or six pounds of silver that he had obtained by barter with the Indians.

The king ordered bread baked and fish prepared in the Indian fashion to feast our Frenchmen. During the repast, he talked of various other kings, his friends and allies, reckoning up to the number of nine of them by name: Cadecha, Chilili, Eclavou, Euacappe, Calanay, Onachaquara, Omittaqua, Acquera, and Moquoso. He said that all of these with himself, and up to the number of more than forty, were vassals of the great King Olata Ouae Outina. Then he started out to list the enemies of Ouae Outina. The first one listed was Chief Satouriona, monarch of the valley of the River of May, who had thirty vassal chiefs under him, of whom ten were his brothers. Because of this he was greatly revered in these parts. Then he named three others not less powerful than Satouriona. The first of these lived a two-day journey from Olata Ouae Outina and made war with him regularly. He was called Potavou and was a fierce man in war. Yet he had pity in the execution of his fury, because when he took prisoners under mercy he was content to mark on their left arm a great sign or brand and then let them go without any further hurt.

Two others named were Onatheaqua and Houstaqua, powerful and wealthy lords, especially Onatheaqua, who lived near the high mountains which are full of many unusual things, including stone from which they make wedges to split wood. It was said that the reason that moved Potavou to make war against Olata Ouae Outina was that he feared that Outina and his companions would take the hard stone from his lands to arm their arrows and that they would not be able to get any at a closer place.

Molona told Captain Vasseur that his ally kings, who were vassals of the great Olata, armed their stomachs, arms, thighs, legs, and foreheads with large plates of gold and silver so that arrows shot at them could not do any damage and would be broken on striking their targets. Then Captain Vasseur asked whether King Onatheaqua and Houstaqua resembled the Frenchmen, because the description that he had heard made him question whether they might be Spaniards; but Molona said no, that they were Indians just like the others, except that they painted their faces black while others like Molona painted theirs red. Then my Lieutenant le Vasseur and my sergeant promised him that later I would go to this place with my brothers, and in alliance with Olata would return victorious from those high mountains. The king was overjoyed by this proposal. He said that the least of the kings that he had named would give to the general of this expedition the height of two feet of gold and silver, which by force of arms they had already taken from the two kings Onatheaqua and Houstaqua.

The entertainment and discussions being finished, my men re-embarked to bring the good news back to me at the fort of Caroline. But after they had sailed down the river quite a distance and were within three leagues of us, the tide was so strong against them that it forced them to land and retire for the night in the dwelling of another chief, named Molona. He showed himself to be delighted at their arrival because he desired to have news of the Thimogona and thought that the Frenchmen had gone there for no other reason than to fight them. Perceiving this, Vasseur dissembled well and made Molona think that he had gone to the Thimogona to conquer them mercilessly by sword, but that since the Thimogona had been alerted, the enterprise had not been a success and the enemy had fled into the woods and saved themselves and that, nevertheless, our Frenchmen had killed a few in hot pursuit who would not now be carrying news to their companions!

The chief was so glad to hear these fabrications that he interrupted him and asked Vasseur how he commenced the battle and how it had been carried out and prayed that he would show by signs how everything was done. Instantly François la Caille, the sergeant of my company, took his sword in hand, saying that with the point of it he had thrust through two Indians who were running into the woods and that his companions had done no less on their part. Then he said that if fortune had continued with them and if they had not been discovered by the Thimogona, the victory they would have had would have been glorious and memorable forever.

Then the chief showed such great satisfaction with this account that he did not know how to thank our Frenchmen, and he insisted that they enter his home for a feast in their honor. He made Captain Vasseur sit next to him in his own chair, which the Indians feel is a great honor. Two of his sons, both with handsome and powerful physiques, sat just below. All the others placed themselves in such order as seemed proper to them. According to their custom the Indians presented their drink of cassena to the chief and then to his closest friends and favorites.

Then the one who brought the cup set it aside and withdrew a little dagger which had been stuck in the roof of the house; and prancing around like a madman with head held high and with great steps, he rushed over to stab an Indian who sat alone in one of the corners of the building, at the same time crying out in a loud voice, "Hyou." The poor Indian did not stir at all from the blow but quietly endured it. The man with the dagger quickly put it back in its former place and began to serve the drink again. He had not done this for long and had scarcely given three or four persons a drink, before he left his bowl again, took the dagger in his hand, and returned to the Indian he had struck before, giving him a very sharp blow on the side and crying out, "Hyou," as he had done before. Then he returned and replaced the dagger in its place, and sat down among the rest of us. A little while after that, the man that had been struck fell down backwards, stretching out his arms and legs as if about to die.

Then the younger son of the chief, dressed in a long white skin and weeping bitterly, placed himself at the feet of the man who had fallen backward. A half of a quarter of an hour afterward two others among his brothers, similarly dressed, came to the persecuted one and began to groan pitifully. Their mother came from another area bearing a little infant in her arms, and going to the place where her sons were, uttered a series of moans and raised her eyes to the sky. She prostrated herself on the earth, crying so dolefully that her mournings would have moved the hardest heart in the world with pity. Yet this was not enough, for then a company of young girls came in, weeping grievously as they went to the place where the Indian had collapsed. Afterwards, as they picked him up, they made the saddest gestures they could devise and carried him away into another lodging a short distance from the hall of the chief. They continued their weeping and wailing for two long hours. Meanwhile, the Indians continued to drink the cassena, but in dead silence, so that not one word was heard in the room.

Le Vasseur was disturbed that he did not understand these ceremonies and asked the chief what they meant. The chief slowly replied, "Thimogona, Thimogona," and said nothing more. Being even more displeased by this meager answer, the captain addressed himself to another Indian, Malica, a brother of the chief and like his brother also a chief. He gave the same response and requested that no more questions be asked on this matter and that Vasseur have patience for the time being.

After a while the crafty old chief asked Vasseur to show his sword. This could not be refused, since it was thought that he wanted to study the nature of the weapon. But the captain realized suddenly that the enquiry was to another end; for the old man, holding it in his hand, looked at it from every angle to see if he could find any blood on it which might show whether any enemies had been killed. Indians usually bring their weapons back in bloody condition to prove their victory. Not seeing any such sign, he was on the point of saying that no Thimogona had been killed, but Vasseur prevented this by showing by signs how he had acted, and adding that by reason of two Indians being slain his sword was so bloody that he had been forced to wash it in the river to make it clean. The old man felt this might be true and made no reply.

Le Vasseur, la Caille, and their companions left the hall to go to the lodging where they had carried the Indian who had been persecuted. There they found the chief eating in Indian fashion as he sat on a tapestry made out of small reeds; and the Indian that had been stabbed was lying near him upon the same tapestry. Next stood the chief's wife and the young girls who had been crying there. These girls warmed piles of moss and used them in lieu of bandages to dress the Indian's side. Then our Frenchmen again asked the chief why the Indian was so persecuted. The reply was that this was simply a ceremony by which these Indians recall the memory of the accomplishments and deaths of their ancestor chiefs at the hands of their enemies, the Thimogona. He said that every time he or any of his friends or allies return from the Thimogona without bringing back the scalps of their enemies or without bringing home some prisoner, he ordered as a perpetual memorial to all his ancestors that the best loved of all his children should be struck by the same weapon by which his ancestors had been killed. This was done to renew the wounds of their death so that they would be lamented afresh. Our Frenchmen being thus informed of the meaning of these ceremonies, thanked the chief for his hospitality, set sail, and returned to me at the fort, where all of this was declared to me as I have written it down here.

On July 28 our ships departed for their return to France.[64] Afterward and about two months after our arrival in New France, Chief Satouriona sent several Indians to ask me if I would make good the promise that I had made when I first came to this country, that is, to show myself to be a friend to his friends and to be an enemy to his enemies and also to accompany him with ample men with guns at the time when he thought it expedient and found occasion and opportunity to go to war. Now, relying on this promise, he requested me not to put it aside, particularly since on the strength of it he had given orders to get an expedition ready, and was now prepared and furnished with all the things that were necessary for the trip. I responded that I would not purchase the friendship of one by the hatred of another, and that even though I wished to assist him I did not have the means to carry it out because at this time it was necessary to make arrangements for food and supplies for the defense of my fort. Also I informed him that my barques were not anywhere near ready and it would take some time to put them in readiness. Finally I said that Chief Satouriona could put himself in readiness to go within two months and that then I would think of fulfilling my promise to him. The Indians told their chief this response and he was not very pleased because he could not defer the execution of the expedition, not only because his foodstuffs were ready but also because ten other chiefs were already assembled with him for this enterprise.

The ceremony which this savage used before he embarked his army is well worth remembering. When he went down to the river bank he was surrounded by ten other chiefs. He promptly demanded that water be brought to him. This being done, he looked up to heaven and began to discuss many things by gestures, showing a great heat in his emotions and shaking his head first one way and then another. Then with a wrath such as I have never seen before, he turned his face toward the direction of his enemies to threaten them with death. He also looked toward the sun, praying for glorious victory over his enemies. Having done these things for at least a half hour, he sprinkled water from his hands over the heads of the chiefs, water which he had taken from a vessel that he held. Furiously he threw the rest of the water on a fire which had been expressly made for this purpose. That done, he cried three times, "He, Thimogona," and was accompanied in this by more than five hundred Indians. They were all assembled there and cried out in unison, "He, Thimogona." According to one of the Indians this ceremony signified that Satouriona begged the sun to give him victory and happiness so that he could scatter the blood of his enemies as he had scattered the water at his pleasure. Moreover it besought that the chiefs who were sprinkled with a part of the water might return with the heads of their enemies, which is the greatest and only measure of their victory.

After Chief Satouriona had completed these cere-

Chief Satouriona, from an ancient drawing by an unidentified artist, on display at the Fort Caroline National Memorial.

monies and had seen to all of his equipment, he embarked and went forward with such speed in his boats that by two hours before sunset on the next day he had arrived in the enemy land, eight or ten leagues from the villages. After all had landed, Satouriona assembled his advisers and it was decided that five of the chiefs would go by the river with half of the forces and would stop at daybreak near the homes of their enemies. As for him, he would go with the rest of the chiefs through the woods and forests as quietly as possible. In this way, all those who went by water and those who went by land would enter the village together at daybreak and cut the enemy to pieces, excepting women and little children.

The agreed plan was vigorously pursued. When it was accomplished, the aggressors took the heads of their slain enemies and cut the hair off, taking a piece of skull with each scalp. They also took twenty-four prisoners and these they hustled off to their waiting boats; when they arrived there, they began chanting praises to the sun, to which they gave credit for their victory. Then they put the scalps at the top of their spears and pushed on to the lands of Chief Omoloa, one of those who was in the company. Arriving there, they divided the prisoners equally among the ten chiefs, first leaving thirteen to Chief Satouriona. He promptly dispatched a runner to give news of this victory to those who had guarded their homes in their absence. These began lamentations, but as night came on they went to dancing and cavorting about in honor of the event.

The next morning Chief Satouriona arrived, and before going into his lodging had all the enemy scalps set up before his door, crowning them with branches of magnolia, thus showing by this spectacle the triumph of the victory he had achieved. At first lamentations and mournings began, but as soon as night came on these changed into celebrations and dances.

After I heard of these things, I sent a soldier to Satouriona, asking him to send me two of his prisoners. This he refused to do, saying that he was not subservient to me and that I had broken my promise under oath, which I had sworn to him on my arrival.

When I understood this from my soldier, who came back speedily, I devised a means of bringing reason to this savage and to make him understand how his bravado would only hurt him. Therefore I told my sergeant to provide me with twenty soldiers to go to the house of Satouriona. I went into his hall without any hesitation and sat down by him and stayed a long time without speaking any word with him or showing him any sign of friendship. This seemed to disturb him, particularly since a number of my soldiers were stationed at the door where I had ordered them not to let any Indian go out. Having stayed there for about a half an hour in this way, at length I asked him where the prisoners were which he had taken from the Thimogona, and I ordered that they be presented to me. The chief, angry in his heart and very much astonished, took a long time to answer this. Finally he told me arrogantly that they were so afraid at seeing us come in such a warlike manner that they had fled into the woods and that they could not be returned now since their location was not known. Then I pretended not to understand what he had said and asked again to receive his prisoners and those of his principal allies. Satouriona then told his son Atore to find the prisoners and to bring them to this place, which he did about an hour afterwards. When they came to the lodging of the chief, they saluted me humbly, and as they raised their hands before me, they would have thrown themselves prostrate at my feet if I had allowed them to do it. Soon afterwards I led them away to our fort.

The chief was greatly irritated by this act and immediately began to think of every possible way by which he could get revenge on us. However, to keep us from having any suspicion and to cover his designs, he regularly sent his ambassadors with presents for us. Among others, he dispatched three Indians to us one day who brought two baskets full of large pumpkins, much better than those we have in France. These Indians promised me in their king's behalf that as long as I stayed in this land I would never run short of food. I thanked them for the good will of their prince and told them of the desire that I had to be useful to Satouriona and his subjects by bringing about peace between him and the Thimogona. I told them that this would be a great advantage, because when he became allied with the kings of that area, he would have open passage against his old enemy, Onatheaqua, against whom he otherwise could not do battle; that Olata Ouae Outina was such a powerful chief that Satouriona alone did not have the means to overcome his forces; but that if they joined together they could easily ruin all their enemies and push their boundaries past the distant southern rivers. The ambassadors asked me to have patience until the next day, when they would return to me after ascertaining the wishes of their lord.

They did not fail in this and gave me to understand that Chief Satouriona was satisfied with the idea. But the contrary was more likely the fact. Satouriona asked me to act promptly, promising to observe and carry out everything that was to be done in his name with the Thimogona. These same ambassadors told these things to the prisoners whom I held. After the ambassadors were gone, I resolved two days later to return the prisoners to Olata Ouae Outina, where they belonged. Before I let them embark, I gave them several trinkets, such as little knives and tablets of glass containing a nice picture of Charles IX. They thanked me for these and also for the kind treatment that I had given them at the fort of la Caroline. Then they embarked with Captain Vasseur and with Lord d'Arlac, my ensign, whom I sent to live for a time with Olata Ouae Outina, hoping that the good will of that great chief would greatly help me in my future discoveries.[65] I had them accompanied by one of my sergeants and by ten reliable soldiers.

So things moved along, and the hate of Chief Satouriona against me continued. On August 29 there fell on the fort such a stroke of lightning that I think it more worthy of interest and of being recorded than any unusual thing that has yet come to pass, more strange than historians have ever written about. The fields were at that time all green and half covered with water, and yet the lightning in one instant consumed about 500 acres and burned with such a bright heat that all the birds which lived in the meadows were consumed. This thing continued for three days. It left us in wonderment, because we could not guess where all the fire came from. At first we had the opinion that the Indians had burned their houses for fear of us, abandoning their old places. Then we thought that they might have observed some ships in the sea and, following their usual custom, lighted up fires here and there to show that people lived in this land. Finally not being reassured, I decided to send to Chief Serranay to find out the truth. But as I was on the point of sending out a boat to ascertain the facts, six Indians arrived from the land of Chief Allicamany.[66]

On entering, they made a long statement, but first they presented several baskets of corn, pumpkins, and grapes. Then they spoke of the amiable alliance that Allicamany wished to enter into with me. They said he could hardly wait, from day to day, until the hour would come when it would please me to put him in my service. They said that in view of the obedience that he had given me, he found it very strange that I should direct such a cannonade against his dwelling, making many of the green prairies burn away right up to the waterline, so much so that he expected to see the fire in his house. Because of this he humbly begged me to order my men not to shoot any more toward his lodging, otherwise he would have to abandon his land and go to a place more distant from us.

When we heard the foolish opinion of this man, which might nevertheless be very profitable for us, I spoke expediently as to what I thought of the matter at that time, responding to the Indians with a happy countenance and saying that what they had told me of the obedience of their chief was very agreeable

with me because previously he had not behaved himself in that way toward me, especially when I had
told him to send me the prisoners that he detained
of the great Olata Ouae Outina, even though he
[Satouriona, i.e., Chief of Allicamany] counted them
unimportant. I told him that this was the principal
reason why I had sent the cannonade, and not that
I had wanted to reach his house, as I could easily
have done that if I had wanted to do so. I said that
I had been content to fire just halfway down the course
to let him know of my power. I assured him that if
he continued in his good behavior, my men would
not be shooting at him in the future and I would be
his loyal defender against his greatest enemies.

The Indians were content with this response and
returned to reassure their chief who, notwithstanding
this reassurance, kept away from his home and at a
distance of about twenty-five leagues for a period of
about two months. At the end of three days the fire
was entirely extinguished. But for two days after that
there was such excessive heat in the air that the river
near which we had our habitation became so hot that
it seemed almost to boil. Many fish died and of many
species, to such an extent that in the mouth of the
river alone there were enough dead fish to fill fifty
carts. The putrefaction in the air bred so many dangerous diseases among us that most of my men fell sick
and seemed about ready to finish their days. However,
our good Lord took care of us and we all survived
without a single death.

Lord d'Arlac, Captain Vasseur, and one of my sergeants had sailed with their ten soldiers about September 10 to take the prisoners back to Outina, naviga-

ting up the river to a place that they discovered by the name of Mayarqua, about eighty leagues from our fort. There the Indians were good hosts to them, just as was the case in many other villages which they visited. From there they went to the lodging of Chief Outina, who, after feasting them as well as he could, asked Lord d'Arlac to stay for a while with his soldiers to make war on his enemy called Potavou. Lord d'Arlac agreed. However, as he did not know how long he would be staying there, he sent Captain Vasseur and the barque back to me with five soldiers.

Now, because it is the custom of the Indians to wage war by surprise, Outina decided to take his enemy Potavou at daybreak; and to bring this about he made his men travel all night. There were about two hundred of them. They were wise in putting our gunbearers at the head of the columns, for, as they said, the noise of the guns would frighten the enemy. They traveled so stealthily that the people of the village of Potavou, twenty-five leagues from Outina's place, were not informed of the imminent attack and suddenly had to defend their village, which was all encircled by woods. They came out in a great company and saw that they were attacked by men with guns, something that they were not accustomed to; and they even saw the leader of their group fall dead at the very beginning of the battle by a blast of the gun of Lord d'Arlac. So they fled, and the Indians of Outina entered the village, taking men, women, and children as prisoners. Thus came the victory of Chief Outina by the assistance of our Frenchmen, who killed many of his enemies and lost in the conflict one of their companions, which greatly grieved Outina.

Eight or ten days afterward, I sent Captain Vasseur with a barque to bring back Lord d'Arlac and his soldiers. On their return they brought me a number of presents from Outina, such as some silver, a little bit of gold, painted skins and other apparel, together with a thousand thanks from the chief, who promised that if in any affair of consequence I had need of his men, he would furnish me three hundred and more.

While I was thus engaged in securing friends and exercising alliances here and there, some of the soldiers of my company were led astray by one Roquette from the country of Perigord. He led them to think that he was a great magician and that by the secrets of magic he had discovered a mine of gold or silver up the river. He swore upon his life that from this mine each soldier could take away the value of 10,000 crowns, without counting more than 1,500,000 which would be reserved for the king. They lined up behind Roquette and behind his confederate, named Genre, in whom I had placed great confidence. This Genre, covetous of becoming rich and wishing to have vengeance on me because I did not let him take a packet back to France, secretly told these soldiers, who were under the domination of Roquette, that I would deprive them of this great gain by requiring them to work every day at the fort without sending them out to explore the countryside. He said everything would be all right after it had been explained to me; and that if I did not give in to their greed, they would find means to get rid of me and to elect another captain in my place. Genre himself brought me the word, telling me how anxious the soldiers were for me to lead them to the lands of the mine. I responded that all of us could not go, and that it was necessary first to put our fortress in such a state that those who remained would be secure against the Indians who might mount a surprise attack. Their manner of reasoning seemed strange to me, inasmuch as they imagined that the king had set up this voyage to make them rich upon their arrival, and they seemed much more interested in their own greed than in service to the king.

But since they saw my response was just toward making the fort more secure and defending it, they plotted mutiny while they were at their labors. They made a flag of old linen which they carried to their work on the ramparts, and they were always armed. I thought all of this was to give themselves a sense of security while they worked; but I discovered afterwards, and even by letters of confession to me from Genre, that these "gentle" soldiers intended to kill me, and my lieutenant also, if I should speak harshly with them at some later time.

About September 20, as I returned from the woods to put the finishing touches on the fort, I was ahead of them on the road, this being my custom to give courage to my soldiers; and I overdid myself in some way, fell sick and thought I would die. During this sickness I often called Genre to my side as he was one in whom I had placed trust and of whose conspiracy I knew nothing at all. He was busy assembling his accomplices to counsel with him, sometimes in his chamber and sometimes in the woods, and he spoke of electing another captain instead of me and of putting me to death. But not being able to put his evil design into effect in the open, he talked to my apothecary, asking him to place in the medicine that I would have

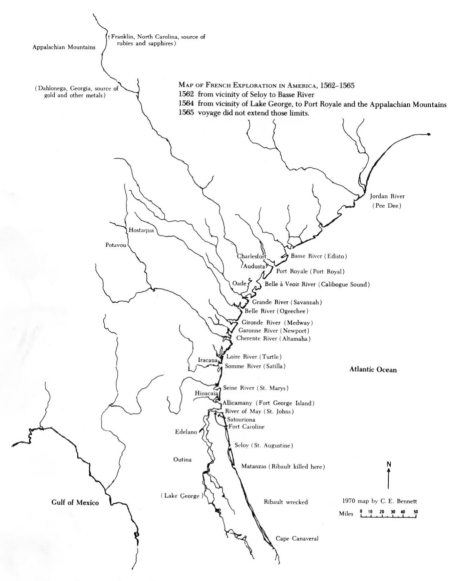

Map of French exploration in America, 1562–1565, by Charles E. Bennett.

to take in a day or two some drug that would cause my death; or at least to give him some arsenic or mercury chloride which he could drop into my beverage. But the doctor turned him down, as also did Mr. S., master of arms.

Finally, being frustrated in these two efforts, he plotted with a few others to hide a barrel of gunpowder under my bed and, by a trail of powder, to blow it up. The gentleman whom I planned to send back to France, and who wished to leave this place, advised me of these enterprises and said that Genre had given him a scandalous ledger containing all kinds of false charges and allegations against me, Lord d'Ottigni, and the other leaders of my company.

Because of this I called all the soldiers together, and also Captain Bourdet with all his company.[67] He had arrived in the roadstead on the fourth of September and had then come into the river. In their presence I had the ledger read aloud so that they could testify to the falseness of what was written against me. Fearing capture, Genre fled to the forest, where he lived for a while with the savages, and with my permission. He wrote to me often and in many of his letters confessed to me that he deserved death. He condemned himself to me and put himself entirely on my mercy and pity.

On November 7 or 8, after I had made provisions for the necessary foodstuffs, I sent two of my men, La Roche Ferrière and another, toward King Outina to explore the countryside there. In the space of five or six months, they discovered many villages and among them one named Hostaqua.[68] The king of this place desired my friendship and sent me a quiver made from wolfskin, full of arrows, a couple of bows, four or five skins painted in Indian fashion, and a silver chain weighing about a pound. In return I sent him two complete sets of clothes, together with some cutting hooks or axes.

About the tenth of the month,[69] Captain Bourdet decided to leave me to return to France. Then I asked him, or rather strongly urged him, to take back with him seven or eight soldiers whom I could no longer trust. He did this as a favor to me but would not accommodate Genre, who offered him a large sum of money to carry him back to France. He took Genre only to the other side of the river.

Three days after his departure, thirteen sailors whom I had brought from France and who were misled by certain other sailors whom Captain Bourdet had left with me, stole away with my barques in the following manner.[70] These sailors of Captain Bourdet said to my sailors that if they had barques like mine they could make a great profit in the Antilles, so they plotted as to how they could steal them. They decided that when I sent them to go into the village of Sarravahi they would not return. This village was about a league and a half from our fort and on an arm of the river. It had been my custom to send them there each day to get clay for brick and mortar for our houses. They gathered up food as best they could and planned to get into one barque and be on their way. And this indeed they did.

What was still worse was that two Flemish carpenters, whom Bourdet had left me, pulled away with the other barque, and before they left they cut the cables of the barque and the small boat of the *Breton* so that they would float away on the tide and I could not go after them. So I was left without either barque or small boat, and this was indeed an unlucky circumstance, because I was already prepared for an exploration of the river.

I understood afterwards that the sailors captured a Spanish passenger barque near Cuba in which they found some gold and silver, which they also seized. And having this booty, they lay about at sea until their food ran out. Because of famine they went to Havana, the principal city in Cuba, whereupon a mischief occurred which I will talk about later.[71]

When I saw that my barques did not return at their accustomed time and suspected what might have happened, I told my carpenters to make a little flat-bottomed boat right away, so I could try to discover in the rivers something of what had happened to the sailors. The boat went out within a day and a night because my carpenters found planks and other wood ready to saw up in accordance with my usual commands to my artisans to keep such available. I sent out men to find news of the thieves, but the search was in vain.

I decided then to build two large barques, each to have thirty-five to thirty-six feet at the keel. These went forward promptly because of the diligence I imposed on the workmen. But greed, being mother of all mischief, took root in the hearts of four or five soldiers, since all of this work and effort did not please them. From then on Fourneaux, La Croix, and Estienne le Genevoys (the three leaders of the sedition), and others began to talk around among the rest of my company, telling them that it was a vile and improper thing for men of position, as they were, to belittle themselves with this common and lowly work, particularly since they had at hand an excellent opportunity to make themselves rich. They said this opportunity was to arm the two barques which they were building and fill them with good men, and then navigate to Peru[72] and the Antilles, where each soldier could enrich himself by 10,000 crowns. And if this should be found bad in France, they could always retire to Italy, since they would be wealthy. At least they could retire there until the furor had subsided, and probably some war would occur and make everybody forget about the whole matter anyway.

That word about riches sounded so good in the ears of my soldiers that, after they had thought it over, their group grew to sixty-six. To give color of right to their plan to steal, they presented me with a request through François de la Caille, sergeant of my company, containing mostly a complaint of scarcity of food to maintain us until ships could return from France. To remedy this they proposed to send to New Spain, to Peru, and to all the islands around; and they asked my permission. I responded to them that when the barques were finished I would have everything in order, that by means of the trading materials sent by the king, to say nothing of my own possessions, we would get enough foodstuffs from the inhabitants of the countryside by trading with them, and that, anyway, we had enough right then for another four months.

I greatly feared that under the pretext of searching for food they would undertake some enterprise against subjects of the king of Spain, something that might properly be laid at my feet, considering that on our departure from France the queen had expressly commanded me to do no wrong against the subjects of the king of Spain nor anything by which he might conceive any unhappiness.[73]

They pretended to be satisfied with this response, but eight days afterward, as I continued to work on our fort and on our boats, I fell sick. Then the plotters so forgot all honor and right-thinking that they decided they now had the opportunity to execute their mutiny. They commenced anew to put into effect their original design, handling their business so well during my sickness that they openly stated that they would seize the guardhouse and myself if I would not consent to their depraved wishes. My lieutenant, on being advised of this, told me about it and said that he had the opinion that some evil thing was imminent. The next day in the morning I was saluted at my gate by soldiers apparently lying in wait to do me a foul deed. I told them to send me two gentlemen in whom I had complete faith, and these two reported to me that the soldiers had come to make a request. I told them that what they did was not the way to present a request to a captain. I said that to do that they should send a few men to make known what they wanted. Then the five principal authors of the sedition, armed with body armor and cocked pistols, entered my chamber and told me they wanted to go to New Spain in search of adventure. I remonstrated with them that they should carefully consider what they were about to undertake, but they responded quickly that everything had been thought through and that I must grant their request. Then I told them that since I was forced to do this, I would send with them Captain Vasseur and my sergeant, who would answer to me and render to me a report of everything that took place on the voyage, and that they should take one man out of every barracks to accompany Captain Vasseur and my sergeant.

Cursing, they replied that they were going, and that nothing remained to be done except for me to turn over all the arms in my control so that I could not use the arms against them, since I would not assist them. But they finally took everything by force and carried it out of my house after they had injured a gentleman in my chamber who had tried to reason with them. They seized me bodily, sick as I was, and carried me prisoner to a ship which was at anchor in the middle of the river.[74] There I remained for fifteen days, attended by one man. They would not let any of my servants visit me or any of the others who took my part in this, and they took away all their arms and armor. They sent me a passport to sign, telling me, after I refused to sign it, that if I made any difficulty they would come aboard and cut my throat. So I finally signed their leave-taking and provided them certain mariners, with Trenchant, an honest and skillful pilot.

The boats, being completed, were armed with munitions of the king: powder, iron balls, artillery, and everything they needed. And they elected as their captain one of my sergeants named Bertrand Sonferrent, and for their ensign one named La Croix. They compelled Captain Vasseur to give them the flag of his ship. Then they decided to sail to Leauguave,[75] a Spanish-owned place in the Antilles, to land there on Christmas night, to go into the church while midnight mass was being said, and to massacre all those who were found there. With this intention they set sail on the eighth of December.

But since the greater part of them soon repented this enterprise and since they started to have mutinies among themselves even before they left the mouth of the river, the two barques separated from each other, with one going along the coast to make an easy journey by the cape to the vicinity of Cuba and the other going straight to the Lucayes Islands. For this reason they did not come together again for six weeks after their leaving.[76]

During this time the barque which had gone by the coast and which was commanded by d'Orange, one of the principal mutineers, and with Trenchant as the pilot, took a brigantine near Arcahaie.[77] The ship was laden with a quantity of cassava and a small quantity of wine. This cassava is a kind of bread made from roots, and it is very white and good to eat. This capture was not made without some loss of life on their part; for in one assault that the inhabitants of Arcahaie made on them, two of their men were taken, namely Estienne Gondeau and one named Grandpré; and two others were killed, Nicolas le Maistre and Doublet. Nevertheless, they took the brigantine and removed to it all the stuff that was in their own barque, because it was a larger ship and with better sails than their own.

Then they sailed right to the Cape of Santa María, near Leauguave, and landed there to caulk and strengthen their boat, which had shipped a quantity of water. Then they decided to go to Baracoa, which is a village on the Isle of Jamaica.[78] On arrival, they found a caravel of fifty or sixty tons in the harbor, and they took it empty. They celebrated in the city for a period of five or six days and then sailed off in this boat, abandoning their second one and sailing to the Cape of Tiburon.[79] They came across a patache and took it by force after a long battle. The governor of Jamaica[80] was in this patache and a rich cargo with much gold, silver, and merchandise, as well as wine and a quantity of other things. They decided to go prowling again in their caravel and with their governor of Jamaica along with them, but when they arrived at Jamaica they failed to capture a caravel there because it was saved by the harbor.

The governor, upon discovering that he had been taken to the place where he wanted to go and where he was governor, slyly asked that the two little boys who had been taken with him be sent by boat to his wife in the village so that she could return some food.[81] But instead of writing to his wife, he secretly told the boys to tell her that she should bring the ships of neighboring ports to his aid. She followed instructions so carefully that in the morning, about the break of day, as the mutineers were resting at the harbor's mouth, which reaches about two leagues into the land, there came from the harbor a malgualire—a boat which could sail backwards and forwards—and then two great ships, each eighty to a hundred tons, well equipped with artillery and well furnished with men.

Our mutineers were taken by surprise, not having discovered those approaching them, partly because of the earliness of the day, partly because of the length of the port, and partly because they suspected nothing. It is true that twenty-five or twenty-six aboard the brigantine observed these vessels when they were close by, and, not having time to pull in anchors, they cut the cable. And the trumpeter, who was inside, alerted the others. As for the Spaniards, on finding themselves discovered, they sent a volley from their cannon to the broadside of the French; and they pursued the French for three leagues. Finally, they took their ships back to port. The brigantine, having escaped, passed in view of the Cape of Aigrettes and of Cape San Antonio on the coast of Cuba;[82] and from there passed within sight of Havana.

The pilot Trenchant and the trumpeter and some of the other sailors on the brigantine who had been forced on the voyage—as I have already spoken about—desired to rejoin me. To this end they agreed that if the wind would favor them, they would go through the Bahama Channel while the mutineers slept. They accomplished this with such good success that at daybreak on March 25 they were off the coast of Florida. Knowing the wrong that they had done, the Frenchmen pretended to be judges in a type of mockery, but that was only after they had drunk heavily of the wine which remained from their piracy. One pretended to be the judge, another pretended to be myself, and another, having heard the pleas, concluded: "You can make your pleas as good as you wish, but if we arrive at the fort of la Caroline and the captain does not hang you, I will never take him for an honest man." Others guessed that after my anger had subsided I would forget the matter.

Their sail was no sooner discovered along our coast than a king of the place, named Patica, living eight leagues distant from our fort and one of my good allies, sent an Indian to tell me that he had discovered a ship along the coast and that he believed it to be of our nation. So this brigantine, oppressed with famine, came to anchor in the mouth of the River of May. At first we guessed this was a ship coming from France, which would have given us much happiness. But having viewed her more closely, I ascertained that it was our mutineers who were returning. So I sent Captain Vasseur and my sergeant to talk with them and to tell them to bring the brigantine in front of the fortress, which they promised to do. There were about two leagues between the fortress and the place where they had dropped anchor near the mouth of the river. The next morning I sent back to them the same captain and sergeant with thirty soldiers, because I saw that they were delaying their coming.

So the mutineers were brought back; and since some on leaving the fort had sworn never to return, I was glad for them to keep their oath. To this end, I went toward the mouth of the river at the place where I built ships and barques,[83] and told my sergeant that he should bring the four principal authors of the sedition to land there, first putting their feet in irons. It was not my purpose to punish the others, understanding that they had been unduly persuaded and because, following the advices of my council especially assembled on the matter, I had decided that only four should die as an example to the others. In this place I made to them the following statement:

"My friends, you know why it pleased the king to send us to this land. You know that he is our natural prince whom we are commanded by God to obey, and that we are neither to spare our goods nor our lives in being of service to him. You know, or at least you cannot ignore, that, in addition to this general and natural obligation, you have also agreed with him that for reasonable wages and pay you are bound to follow whomever he establishes over you to be your chief and your commander in his name. Having given him, for this purpose, your oath of fidelity, you cannot by any means revoke it because of any temptation that you might have to do anything to the contrary. By this contract you live on his bread, and that is reason enough for you to be faithful. Nevertheless you have been more interested in your misguided pursuits than in your integrity, which invites you to remember your oath. And you have become contemptuous of virtue and have lost your judgment in believing that you could do anything you wanted to do. It comes to this: You may believe you can escape the justice of men, but you cannot escape the justice of God, Who has surely conducted you, in spite of yourselves, to return to this place, and has made you confess how true His judgments are and that He will never allow such an offense to go unpunished."

After I had said those things to them and other things which we had decided upon in council, then, because of the crime that they had committed against His Majesty and against me who was their captain, I condemned them to be hanged. Seeing then that they did not have any door behind them to save them from this fate, they began to pray to God. But one of the four prisoners, hoping to make my soldiers mutiny, said to them, "My brothers and companions, how can you allow us to die so disgracefully?" Taking the words out of his mouth, I told him that they were not companions of his in sedition and rebellion against the service of the king. My soldiers then asked me not to hang them but to permit them to be killed, and then, if I thought it best, their bodies could be hung on some scaffold along the banks of the river's mouth. This I promptly had done.

That was the story of my mutineers. With their exception, we all lived in peace and fulfilled my earnest desire to have a worthwhile and peaceful expedition. But since I have been speaking of nothing but their misadventures and their nautical enterprises while away from us, and of nothing about our fort, I will return to what happened to me during their absence.

First, I gave thought to the causes of the difficulties. These mutinies could not really be founded upon the lack of food, because ever since our arrival each soldier had received each day, up until the day of their confronting me and even until February 28, one loaf of bread weighing twenty-two ounces. But I recollected how all new conquests made at sea or on land were usually beset by internal rebellions, which are easily started because of the great distances from the homeland and because of the hope soldiers have of profiting from them. We are well informed of this by ancient histories, and by what recently happened in the adventures of Christopher Columbus after his first discovery, and by what happened to Francisco Pizarro and Diego d'Almagro in Peru and Hernando de Cortés. A hundred thousand other things came to my mind to reassure and fortify me.

My Lieutenant d'Ottigni and my company sergeant came to get me from the ship where I had been prisoner, and carried me back in a barque as soon as the mutineers had gone. On returning to the fort, I assembled in the plaza in front of the guardhouse all of my company who remained, and recalled to them the crimes that had been committed by those who had mutinied and asked them to remember well that day in order to testify if it should become necessary. I appointed new squad leaders here and there and gave them new orders of the guard because so many of the soldiers in whom I had placed confidence had deserted. My declaration having been made, they promised me with a common accord to give true obedience and to do everything that I commanded, even if it were to die at my feet for the service of the king. In this, truthfully, they did not fail; and after the mutineers left, I doubt there ever was anywhere a captain more strictly obeyed than I.

The next day after my return to the fort I brought my men together again to talk with them about our fort not yet being completed, and I advised them that it was necessary that everyone give a helping hand to protect ourselves against the Indians. They willingly agreed and raised up the wall all along the west side, with turfs from the gate up to the river. That done, I put carpenters to work to make another barque of the same size as the others. I ordered the sawyers to prepare the planks, the smiths to prepare braces and nails from iron, and others to make charcoal; and so the barque was finished in eighteen days. Then I had another one made, but smaller than the first, for better explorations in the river valley.

In the meantime, the Indians visited me and always brought various presents, such as fish, deer, turkeys,

Timucuan owl totem, over four hundred years old, removed from the muck of the St. Johns River near DeLand in June, 1955, now owned by the Fort Caroline National Memorial and on temporary loan to the Florida State Museum at Gainesville.

panthers, little bears, and other things according to the area in which they lived. I paid them with sickles, knives, glass prayer beads, combs, and mirrors.

Two Indians came to me one day on behalf of their king, Marracou, who lived about forty leagues south from our fort on the coast. They told me that there was a man named Barbu in the house of King Onatheaqua, while in that of King Mathiaca there was another man whose name they did not know; but that both men were not Indians. Because of this, they thought that these could be Christians. So I sent word to all the neighboring kings that if any Christians lived in their land and if they could find a means of my recovering them, I would reward them amply. They who loved presents so much took great pains to see that the two men of whom I have spoken were brought to me at the fort. They were naked and wore their hair long, down to their loins, just like savages. They were Spaniards, and they had become so accustomed to the land in which they lived that at first they found our manners strange. After talking to them for a while, I had them clothed and their hair cut. They did not wish to part with their shorn hair, so they wrapped it in a cloth, saying that they would report to their country with this as evidence of the misery they had experienced in the Indies. In the hair of one of them was found a little gold hidden away. Its value was about twenty-five crowns, and he gave it to me.

I talked with them concerning the places where they had been and how they came there, and they answered me that fifteen years earlier three ships had been shipwrecked along a part of the coast of Calos,[84] and that they had been on one of those ships. This was among the sand islands which are called the Martyres.[85] They said the king of Calos had recovered the greatest part of the riches which had been in those ships and that most of the persons aboard were saved, including three or four young married women. They said these women still lived with the king of Calos, together with their children. I asked them about the king, and they told me that he was the strongest and most powerful Indian in the country, a great warrior having many subjects under his sovereignty.

They told me, moreover, that he had a great store of gold and silver enough in a certain village to fill to the brim a hole to the height of a man and as wide as a barrel. The Spaniards said that I could recover all of this if I would march there with a hundred soldiers with guns. They said that I could also get much of the mineral wealth from the common people in that locality, who also had a great store of it. They told me that when the women of that area went to dance they wore around their waists large plates of gold as big as saucers and in such numbers that the weight hindered them in their dancing, and that the men had gold in similar quantities. They said that the greatest part of these riches came out of Spanish ships which went down in these straits and that the rest came from trade which this king of Calos made with other kings in the countryside.

Finally, they said that the king was held in great reverence by his subjects and that he made them believe that his sorceries and spells were the reason why the earth brought forth her fruit; and that to persuade them of this idea he withdrew one or two times each year to a certain house, accompanied by two or three of his closest associates, and there did certain magic deeds. They said if anyone went to see what was done in that place the king had them quickly killed. Moreover, they told me that every year at the time of harvest this barbarian king sacrificed a man[86] whom he kept expressly for this purpose, picked from a number of Spaniards who by ill fortune were cast upon the coast.

One of these Spaniards told me that he had served the king of Calos a long time as a messenger and that on several occasions, by such order, he went to visit a king named Oathchaqua, who lived four or five days away from the land of Calos, and that the king was always his faithful friend. He said that in the middle of the trail there was an island situated in a great lake of fresh water named Serrope,[87] about five leagues in size, and that this island abounded with many sorts of fruit, especially dates from the palms. He said that the Indians made a good trading business from these, but that it was not so great as the business from a sort of root from which they make a flour for bread, and that there is no better bread to eat anywhere. He further said that for fifteen leagues around there the whole countryside is fed with this root, which is the reason why the inhabitants of the island make a great profit from their neighbors, because they will not part with this root without being well paid for it. Moreover, these Indians are held to be the most belligerent of all men, which they demonstrated when King Calos made an alliance with Oathchaqua and was deprived of the latter's daughter who had been promised to him in marriage.

This Spaniard told me about the event as follows:

Oathchaqua was well attended by his subjects when he escorted one of his daughters, an exceedingly beautiful girl according to the standards of that area, to present her as a wife to King Calos. The inhabitants of this island learned of the matter and put up an ambush where they had to pass. Oathchaqua was put in retreat, the maiden captured together with all of her ladies in waiting, and all of them were carried away to this island. This was considered a great victory among the Indians, for afterwards they married these captured maidens and loved them with special devotion. The Spaniard who told me this also told me that after this defeat he went to live with Oathchaqua and had been with him for eight years up until the time that I found him. The land of Calos is situated upon a river which is toward the south and forty or fifty leagues distant from the Cape of Florida.[88] The home place of Oathchaqua is north from the cape and at a place our charts call Canaveral, at 28°.

About the twenty-fifth of January, my neighbor Chief Satouriona sent me some presents by two of his subjects in order to persuade me to join him in making war against Ouae Olata Outina, who was my friend. Satouriona requested me to bring back some of my men who were still with Outina, claiming that if it had not been for them he would have often had an opportunity to attack and defeat Outina. He pled with me by means of other kings, his allies, who for three or four weeks sent messengers to me for this purpose. But I would not consent that they make war upon Outina. Instead, I endeavored to make them friends. So Satouriona and his allies agreed to await what I would finally say. Thereupon the two Spaniards, who understood Indians very well because of their long habitation with them, warned me that in any case I should not trust these Indians, because when they made the best appearances of good will it was then that they were planning a surprise attack and treachery, and that it was natural for them to be the greatest traitors and deceivers in the world. Besides, I did not trust them myself because I had discovered a thousand of their ruses and tricks, from actual experience as well as from the teachings of modern history.

Our two barques were dispatched under Captain Vasseur as I sent him to explore along the coast toward the north and to navigate up there in a river valley where the king was called Audusta, the lord of the place where those of the 1562 voyage had been told to live. I sent the king two outfits of clothes, along with a number of sickles, knives, and other small merchandise, in order to establish his friendship more firmly. And in order to help the progress of the project I sent along with Captain Vasseur a soldier named Aymon, who was one of those who returned home from the first voyage, hoping that King Audusta would recognize him. And before they embarked, I ordered them to inquire about what had happened to another soldier named Rouffi, who had remained alone in that area when Captain Nicolas Masson and those of the first expedition had embarked to return to France.[89]

Our people learned upon arrival that a barque passing that way had carried away this soldier, and afterwards I knew for a certainty that they were Spaniards who had carried him to Havana. King Audusta returned my barque full of corn, together with a supply of beans, two deer, some hides painted in their fashion, and some pearls, of little value because they had been burned. He sent me word that if I would live in his place he would give me a large countryside, and after his harvest of corn he would give me everything that I wished of the crop.

In the meantime, a great flock of doves came to us, unexpectedly and for a period of about seven weeks, so that every day we shot more than two hundred of them in the woods around our fort.

When Captain Vasseur returned, I had the two boats filled with my soldiers and sailors and sent them to carry a present from me to the widow of King Hioacaia, who lived twelve leagues to the north from our fort. She received our men courteously and returned my barques full of corn, acorns, and baskets full of the cassena leaves from which they make their drink. The land of this widow is the most productive in corn of any along the coast, and also the most beautiful. They said that this queen is the most attractive of all Indian women and the one held in the greatest respect. Her subjects honor her so greatly that most of the time they carry her on their shoulders, not wishing to allow her to walk in the paths. And a few days after the return of my barques she sent her haitiqui, that is to say, her interpreter, to visit me.

Believing that we were then supplied with enough food until the ships would return from France, and being anxious to keep my men employed, I sent my two barques to explore along the river and up toward the head of it. They went so far up that they were fully thirty leagues above a place called Mathiaqua, and there they discovered a lake so broad that the other side of it could not be seen.[90] According to reports of the Indians who had mounted the highest trees in the countryside to try to see land on the other side of the lake, they had never been able to see it. This was the reason why my men did not go any farther and why they retraced their steps. In their returning they visited the island of Edelano, situated in the midst of the river and as beautiful a place as any that could be found in the world.[91] In the area of some three leagues that may comprise it in length and breadth, you can observe a great fruitfulness of useful things and a very respectable population. On leaving the village of Edelano to go to the river side, you go through a walkway, about three hundred paces long and about fifty paces wide, lined on each side with great trees. Their branches form an arcade overhead in such a beautiful manner that it seemed that it could be an arbor made for the purpose. It was as beautiful as any that could be found in Christendom, and it was entirely natural.

Our men left there, traveling to Eneguape and then to Chilily and from there to Patica; and finally they came to Coya, where they left their boats in a little branch of the river with men to guard them. They went on to visit Outina, who received them very graciously. When they left his house he begged them so earnestly to stay that six of my men remained with him. One of these was a gentleman named Grotauld. After staying there about two months, doing a good job of exploring with another who had been there for

quite a while for this purpose, he returned to the fort
and told me that he had never seen a more beautiful
contryside.

Among other things that he told me about was his
visit to a place called Houstaqua, where the king was
so powerful that he could command three or four
thousand savages in battle. He said that if I wished
to join up with him we could put everyone else under
our authority. Moreover, this king knew the location
of the Appalachian mountains, where we Frenchmen
very much desire to go and where the enemy of Houstaqua lives. This enemy would be easy to defeat, pro-
viding that we all worked together. This king sent
me several plates of copper taken from this mountain,
at the foot of which there runs a thread of gold or
copper as the savages think.

The Indians dig the sand up with the end of a
hollow, dry reed until the reed is full. Then they shake
it and find among the sands many little grains of copper
and silver. And this leads them to believe that there
would be a major source of metal in the mountain.
Inasmuch as it was not more than five or six days
distant from our fort toward the northwest, I decided
that as soon as our reinforcement should come from
France, I would remove our habitation to some river
further north in order to be nearer to the minerals.

One of my men by the name of Pierre Gambye had
remained a long time before this in this area in order
to learn the language and trade with the Indians. At
last he had come to the village of Edelano, and having
accumulated a quantity of gold and silver, he wanted
to return to the fort. So he asked the king of the village
to lend him a canoe, which is a vessel made entirely

of one piece of wood and used by the Indians in fishing and for going about in their rivers. The king of Edelano agreed, but being jealous of the riches which Gambye was carrying away, he commanded two Indians to be in charge of the canoe and to kill him, returning the merchandise and the gold to the king. This the two traitors brutally accomplished, as they killed him with a hatchet while he fanned a fire trying to cook a fish in the middle of the canoe.

Several days after that, Chief Outina sent word requesting twelve or fifteen of my men with guns to do battle against his enemy Potavou; and he let me know that when this enemy was defeated, he would give me passage and conduct me to the mountains so that nobody could stop me. Then I assembled my men and asked their advices, just as I did in all of my undertakings. Most of them were of the opinion that I ought to give assistance to this king, as I could not undertake the exploration by any better means, observing that the Spaniards in their conquests always entered into alliances, pitting one king against the other.

Notwithstanding this, and because I had always doubted these Indians and because of the recent advice that the Spaniards had given me, I believed that the small number of men that Outina had requested might be in danger; so I sent him thirty men with guns under the command of Lieutenant d'Ottigni. They stayed only two days at Outina's place, during which time the foodstuffs were prepared for the trip. These, according to the customs of the country, are carried by women, young boys, and hermaphrodites.

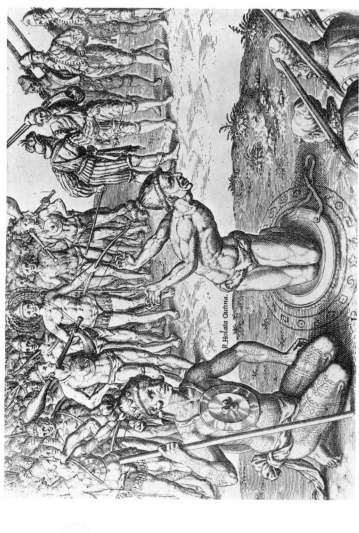

R.Holata Outina.

Chief Outina observing his sorcerer, being the twelfth of the engravings of Jacques Le Moyne de Morgues in his book Brevis Narratio (Frankfort, deBry, 1591).

Outina set out with three hundred of his subjects, each of them with a bow and a quiver full of arrows. They placed our thirty men with guns in the advance guard position. After marching all day, when night came they still had not gone halfway. They lay all night in the woods near a great lake, separating themselves into groups of six, each making a fire around the place where the king slept, who was guarded by the archers most trusted by him.

As soon as day came, they marched forward and to within three leagues of Potavou. There King Outina requested that my lieutenant provide him with four or five men to act as scouts. They departed immediately and had not gone very far when they observed three Indians fishing from a canoe in a lake about three leagues from the village of Potavou. Now the custom is that when they fish on this lake, they always have a guard of men armed with bows and arrows to protect the fishermen. Our men, on advice of those with them, did not go any farther for fear of falling into an ambush. So they returned to Outina, who quickly told them to go back with a stronger force to surprise the fishermen, so that they could not advise Potavou of the arrival of his enemies. They did not accomplish this perfectly, as two of the Indians escaped. The third tried to swim, but he was shot by arrows, dragged ashore, and scalped by our Indians. They cut off his arms on the path, preserving his scalp for the celebration which they hoped to have after the defeat of their enemy.

Outina, fearing that Potavou would be alerted by the fishermen who had escaped and that he might be well prepared against their advance, begged the advice of his jarua, as they call their magician, as to whether it would be wise to go on. This sorcerer made some hideous and terrible signs and used certain ritual words, and when this was ended told the king that it was best not to go on any farther and that Potavou, supported by at least two thousand Indians, was waiting for him. Besides this, he said that all the Indians were furnished with cords to bind up the prisoners whom they would assuredly take. This caused Outina not to wish to go any farther.

My lieutenant was furious because of going through so much trouble without doing anything of importance, and he told the king that he would never have a good opinion of him nor of his men if they would not take the risk; and that if the king did not wish to take it, at least he should be given a guide so that he and his small group could go on to the enemy camp. Outina was ashamed, and because of his high regard for Lord d'Ottigni decided to go forward. He found the enemy at the exact place where the magician had said they would be. The battle began and lasted for three hours. Outina would have been defeated if it had not been for our men with guns, who carried the brunt of the combat and killed a large number of the soldiers of Potavou, routing the rest of them. So Outina was contented for the time being and withdrew his men down the road toward his home. This greatly disgusted Lord d'Ottigni, who wanted nothing more than going on to complete victory.

After Outina arrived at his house, he sent messengers to eighteen or twenty villages of other kings, his vassals, and summoned them to be present at the feasts and dances by which he intended to celebrate the victory. In the meantime Lord d'Ottigni, having rested for two days, took his leave of the chief and left a dozen men to protect against Potavou should he come to burn the houses of Outina in revenge. So d'Ottigni went upon the trail to return to me at the fort; and on his arrival told me everything that had passed, including that he had promised the twelve soldiers that he would go back for them. Then my neighbor kings, all enemies of Outina, seeing that my lieutenant had returned, visited me with presents and to learn how things went, praying that I should take them into friendship and hold Outina as an enemy. I would not agree to their wishes in this for many good reasons.

The Indians are accustomed to leave their houses and retire into the woods for a space of three months, namely January, February, and March, during which time you do not see an Indian anywhere, because during this time they only hunt game and live in little cabins in the woods, living upon what they take in the chase. This was the reason why we could get no foodstuffs from them during this period. I would have been in trouble if I had not stored some provisions, and the men were well supplied until the end of April, which was the time when, at the latest, we expected to have help from France.

This hope of reinforcement was the reason why the soldiers did not take great concern to conserve their foodstuffs, knowing that each day I would distribute to them equally the things I got from the countryside, without reserving anything more for myself than I did for the soldier of the lowest rank in the company. The month of May coming and no assistance having arrived from France, we fell into great need for foodstuffs, and we had to eat roots and a type of sorrel plant that we found in the fields.[92] Even though the Indians had returned by this time, they could not help us except with some fish, without which we certainly would have died. Before this they had already given us the greater part of their corn and beans in return for our merchandise. This famine continued throughout May and through mid-June, during which time the soldiers and workmen wasted away and could not work. They did nothing but go, one after the other, to the lookout at the top of the mountain near the fort, to try to discover some French vessel if they could.

Finally, despairing of all hope, they came together to ask me to give orders that they all return to France, feeling that if we let pass the season of good sailing weather we would not be likely to see our country again. They reasoned that there must be trouble in France, since the assistance promised from there had not been forthcoming. In the end it was decided among everyone that we would fit out the *Breton*, which was commanded by Captain Vasseur. But since this ship was not large enough to hold all of us, some proposed that it would also be a good idea to put two more levels on the brigantine which the mutinous soldiers had brought back; and that twenty-five men should try to make the trip back to France in it. Others said that it would be much better to make a good ship on the foundation of the galley. So I ordered it built, and everybody promised to work hard on it. I asked my shipwrights for advice as to how long it would take for this ship to be ready, and they assured me that it could be done by August 8.[93]

I promptly scheduled the work, telling my lieutenant, Lord d'Ottigni, to obtain the timber necessary for the ships; and my ensign, Lord d'Arlac, to take a barque to a place a league from the fort to cut down trees for planks and to direct the sawyers whom he took with him to saw them up. I ordered my company sergeant to work with fifteen or sixteen men to make charcoal; and gave orders to Master Hance, keeper of the artillery munitions, and to the gunner, to provide the resin to cover the ships with. This work was done so well that within three weeks or less they gathered two hogsheads of resin.

Now only the most important thing remained, which was to obtain enough foodstuffs to feed us during our work. This I undertook to accomplish with the rest of the company and the mariners. To this end I embarked, being the thirtieth of them, and sailed in a large barque to make the voyage of forty or fifty leagues. We were without any food, which shows how low the food supplies at the fort were. True it is that certain of the soldiers were better conservers than the rest, and having made some provisions of acorn meal, they sold a little plate of it for fifteen or twenty sous to their companions.

During our voyage we had nothing to eat but raspberries of a round type, black and tiny, and the roots of palmettos, which we gathered on the river banks. After we had sailed a long time fruitlessly, I returned to the fort, where the soldiers were beginning to be weary of working because of their great hunger. They counseled together and suggested to me that since we could not obtain any more foodstuffs from the Indians, we should capture a subject of one of the kings of the country as hostage for the procurement of foodstuffs. I told them that such a deed should not be attempted in fact before the full consequences of it had been considered. They objected that the time had long passed for help to come to us from France and that since we planned to abandon the countryside there was no longer any danger from making the Indians unfriendly by forcing them to furnish us with food. I would not agree immediately with their suggestion but promised to speedily request the Indians to bring foodstuffs in exchange for merchandise and clothing.

They did this for a space of a few days, during which time they brought their meal and fish, which the mischievous Indians, since they knew of our great hunger, sold to us at very dear prices. For practically nothing they obtained from us every bit of merchandise which remained. To make things worse, fearing to be captured by us and seeing that we had spent everything we had, they would not come within gunshot range from our fort. At that distance they brought their fish in their little boats; and there our soldiers were forced to go. Oftentimes I saw our Frenchmen give the very shirts off their backs to obtain one fish. If at any time they remonstrated with the savages about excessive prices, these villains would answer brusquely, "If you value your merchandise so greatly, eat it, and we will eat our fish." Then they would break into laughter and mock us in derision. Losing patience, our soldiers were at the point of cutting them to bits to make them pay for their arrogance. I took pains to calm down the impetuous soldiers because of the importance of not being in controversy with the savages at that time. I desired to put off that sort of thing as long as possible.

Because of this, I decided to send word to Outina, praying that he deal fairly with his subjects and that we could be helped with corn and acorns. This he did but in a very small amount, sending me twelve or fifteen baskets of acorns and two of pinocqs, which are little green fruit growing in the grass of the river and about the size of cherries.[94] Even this was only accomplished by giving them twice as much as they were worth in exchange. This was so because the subjects of Outina saw clearly the necessity we were in, and had begun to treat us like other Indians. As is easily seen, hard times can change good will among men.

While these things were taking place, there was a little breathing space, because Outina said that he had a vassal king named Astina, whom he had decided to take prisoner to punish him for his disobedience; and he said that if I would give him a number of soldiers for this purpose, he would send them to the village of Astina and in this way I could capture corn and acorns. In the meantime he excused himself from sending any more corn, saying that the little that he had was needed for seed corn. Being somewhat relieved at the hope of his offer, I complied with it and sent the men. They were badly treated because he deceived them, and instead of sending them against Astina, his subject, he made them march against some of his enemies, not vassals. My lieutenant who had charge of this enterprise, with Captain Vasseur and my sergeant, were determined to take revenge on

Latiné	QVERCVS.
Gallicè	GLAND.
Anglicè	ACHORNES·

Acorns, a staple in the diet of the Florida Indians, hence of the French in Florida, depicted here in a woodcut from Jacques Le Moyne de Morgues, La Clef des Champs (London, Blackfriars, 1586).

Outina for this and to cut him up, him and his people; and had they not been afraid of doing something against my will, without a doubt they would have done just that. They did not want to undertake anything else without advising me, and so they returned to the fort, furious and cut to the quick because of the deception which had been played on them. They made their complaints to me and told me that they were almost dead from hunger. They discussed the whole matter with the other soldiers, who were happy that they had not been a party to it. In another meeting they informed me that they persisted in their first decision, which was to punish the audacity and the mischief of the savages, whom they could no longer tolerate. They decided to take one of the kings as a prisoner.

I was constrained to agree with this in order to evade a worse result, the sedition that I saw if I refused them. They asked how I could deny them when I knew the need in which we were and the contempt in which the Indians held us, and they asked if it would not be proper to punish the wrongs that had been done to us in the light of the small amount of respect shown to us. They asked if it were not proper, even aside from the necessity, when the Indians had broken their promises to us.

Having decided to seize the person of Outina, because he had given us occasion to do it and was also most able to provide food, I went out with fifty of our best soldiers in two barques, and arrived in the lands of Outina, at a distance of forty to fifty leagues from our fort. Going ashore, we went to his village about six leagues from the river and there took him prisoner, but not without great cries and alarms being sounded. We led him away to our barques, having first told his father-in-law and his principal subjects that I intended him no harm, but wanted only to relieve the need for foodstuffs which pressed us. I told them that when they supplied me with the food I would talk with them about setting him free and that in the meantime I would return to my barques. I did this because I feared that otherwise they might all get together and some evil might ensue. I was to wait on them there for two days to receive their response, and my meaning was to take the food only in exchange for merchandise. This proposition they promised to consider.

Indeed, that very same evening the chief's wife, accompanied by all of the women of the village, came to the river bank and asked to be able to come to the boat to visit her husband and her son, both of whom we held as prisoners. I discovered the next day five or six hundred Indian archers who were approaching the river bank, calling to me and saying that in the absence of their king, their enemy Potavou had entered their village and burned it to the ground. They asked that I assist them. But in the meantime I easily saw that they had placed one part of their troops in an ambush to capture me if I should come to land. When they understood that I would refuse to do this, they questioned themselves as to whether they had been discovered and tried with every means possible to eliminate the bad opinion that I had of them. Therefore they brought me in their little boats fish and meal made of acorns, and they also made some of their drink called cassena and sent it to me and Outina.

But even though I had gained a point over them, since I still held their king prisoner, I could not get very much food from them at this time, the reason being that they thought that after I had taken the food from them I would then kill their king. This was because they measured my intentions by their own customs, by which they put to death all prisoners captured in war. Despairing of his liberty, they assembled all the people together in a large house and proposed the election of a new king. Then the father-in-law of the king put one of the king's young sons on the royal throne, and he was elected by voice vote. This election was the cause of great trouble among them, because the father of one of the neighboring kings wished to be the ruler and already had a following there. His enterprise was not carried out because, by common consent of the principal advisers, it was decided and ordered that the child of Outina was the logical Indian to succeed his father and that no other had that right.

Now during all this time I kept Outina with me. I lent him some of my clothes to cover him up, and I did the same for his son. His subjects, who had previously had the opinion that I would kill him, became reassured by my good treatment of him and sent two men along the river path to pay him a visit. They brought us some foodstuffs, and on arriving they were treated graciously by me, within the limits of the food that I had. While these things were going on, savages from many adjoining regions came to see Outina and to persuade me to put him to death, offering me, if I would do this, to see to it that I would have no lack of food. There was also my neighbor, King Satouriona, a steeled and able man, very experienced in negotiations. This king sent messengers to me to pray that I would deliver Outina to him. To win me over more easily, he sent to me on two occasions seven or eight baskets of corn and acorns, thinking that in this manner he could bring about an understanding between us. Finally, he saw that it was futile and he stopped sending me ambassadors and foodstuffs. Meanwhile, on account of our short rations, I had difficulties in allotting the work on the ships which we were building for our return to France.

In the end, we were to endure an extreme famine which continued among us through the month of May. In that time of the year neither grain, nor beans, nor acorns were to be found in the villages, because all seeds were being planted; so, we were forced to eat roots. These our men crushed in the mortars which I had brought to make cannon powder and to grind the grain we had brought from other places. Some took the wood of the chinaroot bush, beat it, and made meal of it, which they boiled with water and ate. Others hunted birds with their guns. The misery was so great that I remember one who gathered from among the garbage of my house all the fish bones that he could find, which he ground into a meal for making bread. The effects of this hideous famine clearly appeared among us, for our bones came so close to the skin that most of the soldiers had their skins pierced by their bones in many parts of their bodies. My greatest fear was that the Indians would rise up against us, since it would be very difficult for us to defend ourselves in the extreme weakness of all our forces and with the lack of foodstuffs. Suddenly we came to a complete end of all of our food. Even the river did not have the supply of fish that was usual, and it seemed that land and water fought against us.

Now as we were thus in despair by the end of May and the beginning of June, I was advised by some Indians who were my neighbors that in the high country up above the river there was a new crop of corn, because that country was the earliest to harvest it. This caused me to go up the river with a number of men to a place called Enecaque. I met the sister of Outina there in the village. She was hospitable and gave us fish. We found, as we had been told, that the corn was ripe. But from this good luck something bad came, because the majority of my soldiers fell sick from eating more than their weakened stomachs could digest. During the past four days since we had left the fort we had eaten nothing except pinocqs, which are a tiny fruit, and some fish which we obtained from fishermen we met along the river. And the total food supply was so small in amount that some of my soldiers ate privately the bodies of newborn puppies.

The next day I planned to go to the island of Edelano to take the king, who had killed one of my men, as I have mentioned before. But he was alerted by my departing from my fort and by my course up the river, and so he feared that I was going to revenge the evil that he had done. Consequently, when I came to the place I found all the houses empty because he had fled with his people just a short time before that. I could not restrain my soldiers from burning down the village because of their anger at the murder of their companion.

After leaving there, I went back again by Enecaque, where I gathered as much corn as I could. I took it carefully to the fort to provide for my poor men whom I had left there in such great necessity. They saw me coming from a distance. Because of their great hunger they could not wait until I brought the food to the fort itself, and they ran to the river bank where they thought I would land. When I arrived, I distributed the little corn that I had to each one before getting out of the barque. They showed their extreme famine by eating it before taking it out of its husks.

Seeing clearly the extreme necessity, I made an effort, day in and day out, to seek villages where there might be some food. As I traveled this way and that, two of my carpenters were killed by the two sons of King Emola and by one whose name was Casti. This happened as my men were on their way to a village called Athore. The cause of the murder was that as they walked through the fields of grain, they could not refrain from taking a little, and they were surprised and caught in the act. I was told about this by an Indian who a short time before that had brought me a present from Niacubacany, queen of the village and neighbor of our fort. Upon receiving this news, I sent my sergeant with a number of soldiers who found nothing but the two dead bodies, which they buried. They returned without any further event because all of the inhabitants of the village had fled in fear of being punished for their foul deed.

We were well into the month of May when two subjects of King Outina came to me with a hermaphrodite, to tell me that the grain was ripe in most of their area. Then Outina told me that, such being the case, I should carry him home and he would see that I obtained plenty of corn and beans, and he also said that the harvest from the field which he had caused to be sown for me would be reserved for my use. I took this matter up with others in consultation, and on advice of them all I agreed to the request, since apparently he had the means to give us the foodstuffs which would be necessary for us prior to our departure. I made two barques ready and sailed to Patica, the village about eight or nine leagues from his place. There I found no one because they had all gone into the woods and would not show themselves, even though Outina showed himself. This was because they believed that I would not let him go.

Since they would not come out in the open, I was forced to hazard one of my men who was acquainted with the state of the countryside there; and I delivered through him the young son of Outina and told him to go quickly to the village of Outina and to Outina's father-in-law and his wife and tell them if they wished to have their king returned they should bring me food on the bank of the little river where I was stationed, awaiting them. When he arrived at the village, everyone lovingly caressed the little child and there was no one there who was not happy to touch him. The father-in-law and the wife, hearing the news, ran down the trail toward our barques and brought us bread for my soldiers. They detained me through three days and tried everything they could to capture me. I quickly discovered their intentions and therefore kept careful guard. When they perceived that they could not accomplish their purpose, they told me that they could not give me the foodstuffs because the grain was not yet ripe, contrary to their previous advices. Thus, I had to return to the fort with Outina, where

I had great trouble saving him from the fury of my soldiers, who would have murdered him since they saw how his Indians had deceived us. It seemed that the Indians were content that they had obtained the son, and they did not seem to care greatly about the father.

My hope failing me in this, I decided to send my men to the villages where I thought corn might be ripe by this time. I went out on a number of such trips and pursued this plan for fifteen days. Then Outina begged me to send him back to his village, assuring me that his subjects would have no difficulty in furnishing me foodstuffs. He said if they did refuse me he would be content to have me do to him whatever I wished. I undertook this journey for the second time, with two barques as before. When we arrived at the little river, we recognized the people there who had brought some bread, beans, and fish to give to my soldiers. Nevertheless, they were still holding to their original idea; and they tried by every possible means to entrap me, hoping to make things even by retaking their king and gaining a victory over me. After seeing the little chance that they had to hurt me, they returned to their entreaties and asked if I would send their king with one of my soldiers to the village, suggesting that his subjects upon seeing him would be more inclined to send food. I did not desire to do this because I mistrusted their subtleties, which were not so hidden that there was no ray of light to be seen in them. So I required them to leave two of their men as hostages under the charge that the next day they should bring food. They agreed to this and brought me two men. I put them in chains lest they run away, as I was sure that they had been instructed to do. Four days went by in these negotations, and at the end of them they told me that they could not entirely satisfy me and perform their promises and that the best that they could do at that time was to require that each subject bring his share of grain. They were willing to do this if I returned the two hostages in ten days.

When my lieutenant was ready to depart on this mission, I warned him, above all things, to guard against falling into the hands of the Indians, because I knew them to be very crafty in their undertakings to our disadvantage. He and his group left us and arrived in due course at the small river which we were accustomed to enter in approaching the village of Outina. This was about six leagues from Outina's place. They landed and the lieutenant put his men in military order and marched straight toward the great house which was the king's. There the principal men of the country were assembled, and they ordered a large quantity of food to be brought forth, first by one and then by another, consuming three or four days in the process. By this means they gained time to gather men to ambush us on our retreat. They used many schemes to take us. When they demanded the return of the hostages, our lieutenant would not release them until the foodstuffs had been taken to the barques according to their agreement. Then they said that the women and little children were afraid to see lighted fuses so near to our guns, and they requested that the fuses be quenched so that they might more easily make the people carry the food-stuffs.[95] They promised that they would leave their bows and arrows and let their servants carry them. This second request was given as little attention as the first, because it was easy to see what their designs were.

While these things were taking place, Outina was not to be seen, but kept himself hidden and apart in a little house where certain chosen men of mine went to see him to complain to him of the long delays brought about by his subjects. He answered that his subjects were so incensed against us that it was impossible to make them as obedient as he would have wished and that he could not prevent them, from waging war against Lord d'Ottigni. He also said that even while he was still prisoner and under guard and going through the villages, he saw scalps on arrows stuck up along the edges of the trails, a sure sign of announced war. This was during the time when our men led him through the country to obtain foodstuffs, and the arrows had been brought to our fort by the captain.

Further, Outina said out of the good will that he bore to the captain that he would forewarn the captain's lieutenant that his subjects had decided to fell trees across the little river where the barques were, to bottle them up so that his subjects could easily attack the Frenchmen there. He assured him that for his part he would not be there to meddle in the matter.

What increased the suspicion of war was that as our deputies left Outina they heard the cry of one of my men who was always among the Indians during this journey and whom they did not wish to turn loose until they had obtained their hostages. This poor man screamed in a loud voice because two Indians were carrying him into the woods to cut his throat, but he was immediately rescued. These things having been considered and understood, Lord d'Ottigni prepared to leave on July 27. He put his soldiers in military order and gave each a sackful of grain and was on the trail toward the barques, hoping to forestall attacks by the savages.

On leaving the village there was a great open path, three or four hundred paces in length, covered on each side by tremendous trees. My lieutenant ordered his men into this area and lined them up in the order of march, because he felt sure that if there were to be an ambush it would probably be when they came out from under the trees. So he ordered Lord d'Arlac, our ensign, to march with eight men with guns as a point somewhat before the main troops in order to flush out any danger ahead. Also he ordered one of my sergeants, a corporal, and four gunbearers to march on the outside of the open space, while he himself conducted the rest of the company through it. It happened just as he had predicted, because when Lord d'Arlac arrived at the end of the open space he encountered two or three hundred Indians who met our Frenchmen with a swarm of arrows and with such fury of spirit that it was easy to see how anxious they were to attack us. However, they were so taken back by the response which my ensign and his men gave them that those Indians who fell dead somewhat cooled the ardor of those who remained alive.

My lieutenant had the pace of his men quickened to gain the open ground which I have already described. Then, having gone on about four hundred paces, he was attacked by another group of savages, numbering three hundred; and these assailed him in front while the ones whom he had first met attacked from the rear. The second assault was so sustained that I must say that Lord d'Ottigni performed in defending against it as good a job as was humanly possible for anyone to do. He had need to do it because his opponents were experienced in combat, obedient to their chief, and knowledgeable as to how to conduct themselves in battle; so if d'Ottigni had not provided an answer he would have been in real danger of defeat.

The enemy tactics were that when two hundred had shot their arrows, they retired and gave their places to others who had been in the rear. They were so quick with eye and foot that when they saw a gun laid to the cheek they dropped to the ground, and they jumped up again just as quickly to respond with an arrow. They whirled away if they perceived we were about to take them because there is nothing that they fear more than daggers and swords.

This combat kept up from nine o'clock in the morning until night dispersed them. If it had not been that d'Ottigni had ordered his men to break the arrows which they found on the ground, which were the means of the savages' renewing battle, there is no doubt but that the affair would have lasted longer, because when the arrows gave out the enemy were forced to retire. However, while they fought, they cried out to the effect that they were friends of the captain and the lieutenant and that they fought only to get vengeance against the soldiers, who were their mortal enemies.

My lieutenant, having arrived at the barques, reviewed his men and found that two of them had been killed. One of them was named Jacques Sale and the other was named le Mesureur. He found twenty-two wounded and had them moved to the barques with great care.[96] All the grain that he found among his company came to about the share of two men, which he equally divided among them all. The other grain had been lost when the combat began because everyone was forced to drop his sack to put both hands to work in battle.

During all this time I remained at the fort and kept the work going there, hoping that my lieutenant would fetch us some foodstuffs. As the time passed, I commenced to suspect the truth of what had occurred, which is exactly what I have reported and found out upon their return. Being frustrated from that source, I prayed to God and thanked Him for the grace that He had shown in allowing my poor soldiers to escape. Then I thought of new means to obtain food for our trip to France and to last until the time for our departure. I was advised by some of our company, who regularly went hunting in the woods near the villages, that in the village of Saranai, situated two leagues from our fort on the other side of the river, and at the village of Emoloa, there were fields of ripened grain in a very abundant crop. So I fitted out my barques and sent my sergeant there with a number of soldiers to fetch some, and they did such a good job that they brought back large quantities of grain.

I also sent out toward the river which the Indians call Iracana, named the Somme River by Captain Ribault. When Captain Vasseur and my sergeant arrived there with two barques and their ordinary equipment he found a great assembly of the principal leaders of the place, among whom was Atore (son of Satouriona), Apalou, and Tacadocorou. They had come together to have a good time, because that is the place where the prettiest girls and women of the countryside are. Captain Vasseur tendered presents from me to all of the leaders, to the queen, and to the girls and women of the village. After our men were given as good a time as could be arranged, the barques were quickly loaded with corn. The queen sent me a gift of two small mats which could not have been more artfully made.

Having by these means furnished ourselves with enough provisions, all of us commenced, each according to his ability, to work as diligently as the desire to see our native country moved us. But because two of our carpenters had been slain by the Indians, as heretofore mentioned, Jean de Hais, the master carpenter and a very worthy example of his vocation, came to me and told me that for lack of experienced men he could not put the ship in perfect shape in the time that he had promised. This made our soldiers so furious that they almost killed him. I appeased them as well as I could, and decided to put aside work on that ship and content ourselves instead with putting the brigantine in shape, as I had already orderd.

We began to tear down the houses which were outside the fort and made carbon by burning the wood from them. The soldiers even tore down the palisade on the water side, and I was not able to dissuade them from doing it. I, myself, had decided to destroy the fort before we left and to put it to fire to prevent some newcomer from using it.

All of us were very sad to leave this country in which

we had endured so many hardships and deprivations in order to explore it, only to lose it through the default of our own countrymen. If we had been re-enforced at the time and place promised, the war which we had with Outina would not have occurred and we would not have antagonized the Indians. I had taken such pains to bind them to us by good friendship, gifts of merchandise, clothes, and promises of better things to come, that although I sometimes had to take foodstuffs in a few villages, yet I did not lose the alliance of the eight kings and chiefs who were my neighbors; and they always gave me every possible assistance. This was the principal object of my purpose: to win them and be friendly with them, knowing how their friendship could be important to our plans, particularly while I explored the country and sought to strengthen myself by building the fort.

I leave it to your thought to consider how much it cut us to the heart to leave this place of abundant natural resources, which we knew so well, in coming to which for the services of our country we had left behind our homeland, wives, children, parents, and friends, passing through all the perils of the sea and finally arriving here as a culmination of our great desires.

As each of us tortured our spirits in these or similar thoughts, I spied four sails at sea on August 3 as I walked on a little mountain. This made me very happy and I quickly sent one of those who was with me to alert those at the fort. They were so overjoyed that they laughed and jumped around as if they were out of their minds. After these ships had cast anchor, we saw that they were sending one of their barques to land, whereupon I caused one of mine to be armed and sent to meet them in order to find out who they were. Fearing that they might be Spanish, I put my soldiers in order and in readiness to await the return of Captain Vasseur and my lieutenant, who had gone to meet them. They brought back word that they were English and that they had in their company Martin Atinas of Dieppe, then in their service. He came on behalf of Master John Hawkins, their general, to request that I might give them fresh water, for which they had a great need. He told me that they had been coasting about the shores for a period of about fifteen days searching for fresh water. He brought me from the general some wheat bread and two flagons of wine, which made me feel very good because I had not tasted a drop of wine in over seven months. All of it was divided among the greatest part of my soldiers.

This Martin Atinas had guided the English to our coast, which he knew because of his having come here with me in 1562. It was for this reason that the general had sent him to see me. After I signified my agreement to his request, he passed the information on to the general, who on the next day brought one of his small ships into the river. Then he came to see me in a large barque, accompanied by well-dressed and unarmed gentlemen. He sent for a large supply of bread and wine to distribute among all my men. For my part, I made our guests as cheerful a welcome as was possible and had certain sheep and poultry killed, which to this hour I had carefully guarded in the hope of using them to stock the countryside. Notwithstanding all the need and sickness that had come to us, I had not allowed one chicken to be killed;

and by such effort we had gathered together more than a hundred of them.

Three days passed while the English gentleman remained with me, and during this time Indians came in from every side to look at him; and they asked if he were my brother. I told them that this was so and advised them that he had come to see me and to give me assistance with a large quantity of foodstuffs, so that thenceforward I would not need to take any from them. The news was quickly passed around in the countryside, and ambassadors came to us in the name of their kings, desiring to make an alliance with me, even those who had formerly wished to go to war with me. They declared themselves my friends and servants, and I received them and gave them a few presents.

The general quickly understood the desire and necessity which I had to return to France, and he offered to take me and my entire company; but I would not agree, being in doubt as to why he was so liberal in his treatment. I did not know how things stood between France and England; and even though he promised to put me in France before going on to England, I feared that he might want to do something in Florida in the name of his queen. So I flatly refused his offer. This caused a great murmur among my soldiers, who said that I wanted to kill them and that the brigantine of which I have spoken before was not capable of taking them when the weather of that time of year was considered. The dissension and talk built up more and more when, after the general had returned to his ships, he told some of the gentlemen and soldiers who went to see him off that he greatly doubted that we would be able to make it in the ships which we had, and if we tried it we would no doubt be in great peril. The general said that, if I wished it, he would take part of the men with him and that he would leave a little ship for the transportation of the others.

The soldiers had no sooner come back than they told their companions about this offer, and they quickly came together and advised me that if I would not accept the proposition they would go and leave me behind, because they wanted to accept this promise of transportation. They assembled themselves and came to my chamber and told me what they intended to do. I told them that I would give them an answer within an hour. So then I called together my principal advisers who, after having understood the matter, answered me with one voice that I could not refuse this offer or turn our backs on this opportunity. They said that my actions in accepting God's aid could not be found bad by people in France who had abandoned us.

After much further discussion of this proposal, I advised them that it would be proper to pay for the ship which he would leave us, and that for my part I would be happy to give him the best of my personal possessions—and the little silver that we had collected in the countryside. Then it was decided that the silver should not be given for fear that the queen of England might be encouraged later to take this land, since she already wished to do that, and that it would be better to take the silver to France to encourage our leaders to establish something important for our own nation. It was further decided that since we were going to leave, it would be better to part with our artillery, which in any event we were going to have to leave behind or bury because the feebleness of our men made it impossible to load these things aboard ship.

Having been advised and having decided, I went to the English general, accompanied by Captain Vasseur, Captain Verdier, Pilot Trenchant, and my sergeant, all men experienced in such affairs and sufficiently knowledgeable to make the arrangements. We then visited the ship which the general was willing to sell. He was so reasonable that he took the advice of my men that it was worth seven hundred crowns. To this we amiably agreed. Then I gave to him, as pay, two large cannon, two medium-sized cannon, a thousand pounds of iron, and a thousand pounds of powder.

Having made the bargain, he thought of our personal needs, since we had not lately had anything to eat but grain and water; and being moved by pity, he offered to assist me with twenty barrels of meal, six small barrels of beans, a small barrel of salt, and about one hundred-weight of wax for making candles. Since he saw my soldiers were barefooted, he offered fifty pairs of shoes, which I accepted at a price agreed upon between us. I signed the paper of indebtedness for this and am to this very moment still obligated for it.[97] He did more than this: specifically, he made a present of a large jar of oil, a jug of vinegar, a cask of olives, a large quantity of rice, and a barrel of white biscuits. He also made a number of presents to the principal officers of my company, according to their rank. I must say that we received as many courtesies from this general as it would be possible to receive from any living man. He certainly acquired with us the reputation of being a kind and considerate man, deserving to be recognized by all of us as having saved our lives.

As soon as he had gone, I put my men to work making biscuits from the flour that he left us and fixing barrels to carry the water that would be necessary for the voyage. You can imagine how actively we worked because of the great desire we had to be on our way. So by August 15 we had made such headway that the biscuits, the greater part of our water, and all of the baggage of the soldiers had been put aboard. We had now only to wait for favorable winds which would carry us back to France. If these winds had come as we desired them, we would have been spared much misery; but that was not the pleasure of God, as we will see hereafter.

Being then ready to sail, we decided that it would be good to take a few Indians, men and women, to France, so that if a return voyage were to be made, they could tell their kings of the grandeur of our king, the excellence of our princes, the abundance in our country, and the fashions of life in France; also to the end that they could understand our language to aid us afterwards. So I put things in order and developed a plan to bring the handsomest persons in this country to France, if our intentions had succeeded as I hoped they would. Meanwhile, the neighboring kings came to see me and to visit with me. After they understood that I was going to France, they asked if I planned to return to Florida and if the visit would be brief. I told them that within ten months I would return and visit them again with such strong forces that I could make them victorious over all enemies. They requested me not to tear down my house and to prevent my soldiers from tearing down the fort and their houses, and asked that I leave them a barque with which they could make war against their enemies. I gave them to understand that I would grant their wishes, to the end that I could live there as their friend at least until the moment of departure.

The Third Voyage of the French to Florida, Made by Captain Jean Ribault

WHILE all of this was happening, on August 28 the wind and the sea came through in good shape for setting sail. Captain Vasseur, who commanded one of my ships, and Captain Verdier, who commanded the other, were just about ready to go when they spied sails at sea. They quickly told me of this, and I ordered a barque to be well armed to reconnoiter and discover who these men were who came to us. I sent word to the sentinels who were on our little mountain to have some men go up in the highest trees in order to get a better view. They saw the large barque of the ships, which were still not recognizable. They said, that if they could judge correctly this barque seemed to be chasing my barque, which had just passed the

Fort Caroline, as depicted in Arnoldus Montanus, De Nieuwe en Onbekende Weereld (Amsterdam, J. Meurs, 1671).

bar outside the mouth of the river. It was not then possible to decide whether these were enemies who would carry her away with them. It was just too great a distance to judge accurately.

Being in this doubt, I put my men in order with their battle equipment, to be prepared in case those who came were enemies. Actually I had good reason to do this because my barque went to their ship about two o'clock in the afternoon and yet sent me no news throughout the entire day to reassure me as to who these people were. The next day, at about eight or nine o'clock in the morning, I saw seven barques, including mine, enter the river, each full of soldiers carrying guns and armor, and coming in battle formation along the shore where the sentinels were. They gave no response to the sentinels in spite of all the demands that were made on them to do this. Finally, one of my soldiers fired a round. It did no harm because of the great distance between him and the barques. This event having been reported to me, I sent each man to his battle position and made plans for defense against persons I believed to be enemies. I even placed the two small cannon which still remained with me in such a manner that these people would have received a volley if they had not cried out that Captain Ribault had arrived.

Later I learned why they entered in this manner. It was because of false reports which had been made to Admiral Coligny by some who had returned to France in our first ships. They had given the impression that I had acted grand, played the king, and would resist anyone coming there except under my command. See how the character of good men is often attacked by people who, not having earned credit themselves, try to tear down the work of others, hoping by this to strengthen their own weak courage.[98] This is one of the most notable dangers that come to a commonwealth, and particularly so among men of war who are placed in responsibility. It is very difficult, almost impossible, in commanding a body of men brought together from various nations, such as we have in our wars, yes, I say it is impossible to evade having among them people of bad disposition, who are difficult to manage and who easily conceive a hatred against the commander because of corrections made for the purpose of military discipline. It takes but a small occasion founded on a slight pretext for them to put into the ears of superiors any complaints they have contrived against those whose execution of justice is painful to them. Although I would not put myself among the ranks of the great and renowned captains who have lived in past ages, yet we can judge by their examples how false talebearers have been hurtful to nations. I will cite only Alcibiades as an example from the country of Athens. By this means he was required to be exiled and the citizens of Athens suffered because of it, to the extent that finally they called him back and recognized their mistake in having failed to remember his service and in paying attention to a false report rather than considering his many notable deeds.

And so that I will not be lost in pursuing this course of justification, I come back to the principal subject. Being advised that it was Captain Ribault who had come, I went out of the fort to meet him and to do him all possible honor. I had him saluted with artillery and by my soldiers shooting their guns, and he responded similarly. He came to land and was received with honor and delight as I brought him to my lodgings. I was particularly happy because there were in his company many of my old friends; and I entertained them as best I could with such food as I could get there in the country, and from the small store remaining from what I had obtained from the English general.

I was surprised when all at once everybody was speaking to me about as follows: "My Captain, we thank God that we have found you alive and moreover that the reports that we have heard of you are not true." This sort of talk aroused my curiosity so that I wanted more information promptly, suspecting some evil aspect. Having caught the attention of Captain Jean Ribault, we went aside and outside of the fort together and he told me of the instructions which he had concerning me. He asked me not to return to France but to stay there with him, both myself and my company, and he assured me that he would make it work out all right. I replied that in any other place I would do him all possible service, but that for the present I could not and should not accept his offer, since he had come here to take the place that I had held and that it would be a rebuke for me not to be in command any longer. I said that my friends would not like it and that he himself would not counsel me to do that if I were to ask his advice. He told me that he would not be in command over me, that we could be companions and that he would build another fort, since there would be a need for it, and that he would leave me mine. Notwithstanding this, I told him that I could not have received grander news than that I could return to France; and moreover, if I should stay it would be necessary that one of us have command and the title of lieutenant of the king and that we would not be able to agree on that. I said that I would rather be considered the most wretched beggar in the world than to be commanded in a place where I had endured so much in my duty, unless it were by some great lord or knight of the order. For these reasons I quickly asked him to give me the letters that the admiral had written me. He did this and the contents of these were as follows:

"Captain Laudonnière, because some of those who have returned from Florida speak indifferently about the land, the king desires your presence to the end that with your advice he will decide whether to make a great effort there or to drop the matter. And to this end I send you Captain Jean Ribault to be governor there, to whom you will deliver all that you have in your charge and inform him of all of your explorations."

And in a postscript to the letter there was written:

"Do not think that since I send for you I do so by reason of any discontent or mistrust of you; but it is for your good and credit, and I assure you that during my life you will find me a good commander. Chastillon."

Now, after I had talked with Captain Ribault for some time, Captain la Grange accosted me and told me of numerous bad reports made against me. Among things that he told me was the fact that the admiral took it badly that I had a brought a woman with me; likewise that I desired to play king and had become a tyrant; that I was too hard on the men who had come with me; that I wished to be advanced by some route other than the admiral; and that I had written to a number of lords in the court, a thing that I ought not to have done.

I answered that the woman was a poor chambermaid whom I had brought from an inn to take care of my household business and to care for the domestic animals, such as the sheep and chickens which I brought over to establish in this land; that it was not a reasonable thing to put these household responsibilities in a man's hands; that, considering the length of time that I had to be in this country, it seemed to me that it would not give offense if I brought a woman along to act as a nurse for the soldiers in their sickness as well as for my own sicknesses, such as those I afterwards experienced; that, as an indication of how necessary her services were and how well she was esteemed by each of the men, there were at one time as many as six or seven who asked me for her hand in marriage (One of them, in fact, did marry her after I returned); that, concerning the charges that I tried to play king, these reports were founded on my determination not to let anything happen which was contrary to the fulfillment of my orders and to the service I owed the king; that, moreover, in such circumstances, a governor must make himself understood and must lead, otherwise everyone would see himself as in charge, being so far removed from stronger discipline; and that if the talebearers had called this regimentation, it came more from their disobedience than from my nature, I being less inclined to sternness than they to rebellion.

As to the rest, I answered that I had not written to any of the lords of the court without the advice and order of the admiral, who told me on our departure that I should advise the lords of the council of some of the things that I found in this land so that they would be moved by this to persuade the queen to support this enterprise; that having been but a short time in this country and always being busy building our fortification and unloading my ships, I had not obtained any important new or rare things to send them and thought it best just to advise them in the meantime by letter until, after a longer time here, I could find something to send to them; that the distribution of these letters I had intended to rest only with the pleasure of the admiral; that, if the courier forgot himself to the extent that he had broken the covering of the letters and had presented them himself for hope of gain, it was not by my order; and that I never revered any man more than the admiral, nor had I given any man more willing and faithful service than I gave to him and neither had I tried to advance myself through any other person. This is how things went that day.

The next day Indians arrived from everywhere to know who these men were, and I explained that these were those who came in 1562 and erected the stone which was at the entrance of the river. Some of them remembered Ribault, because he was easy to recognize on account of his great beard. He received many presents from those coming from adjoining villages. Among these he recognized some. The kings Omoloa, Saranay, Allicomany, Malica, and Casti came to visit him and welcomed him with presents according to their custom.

I told them that he had come from the king of France to live there in my place and that I had been sent for. Then they asked him if he would like to present to them then the merchandise he expected to give them later on; and they promised that in a few days they would take him to the Appalachian mountains where they had agreed to take me and that if they did not fulfill this promise, they would be willing to be cut to pieces. They said that there one could find red copper, which in their language is called "sieroa pira," meaning red metal. I had a piece of it and I immediately showed it to Captain Ribault, who had it studied by his goldsmith. He reported that it was, in fact, pure gold.

During these talks and the goings and comings of the kings, I, being worn out with the preceding work that I had been engaged in and depressed by the false rumors that had been spread about me, fell into a great and continual fever which lasted eight or nine days. During this time Captain Ribault brought his foodstuffs to land and placed most of it in the house which my lieutenant had built about two hundred paces outside the fort. He did this to give better cover to them; and also to place the flour close to the bakery, which I had purposefully built out there in order to avoid the danger of fire, as previously mentioned.

But see, how often misfortune searches us out and pursues us even when we think that everything is going just right. Look at what happened on September 4 after Captain Ribault brought up three of his small vessels into the river. Six great Spanish ships arrived in the roadstead where four of our greatest ships still rested. The Spaniards cast anchor and assured our men of friendship and asked about how all our leaders were and named them by Christian names and surnames. I suggest to you that it must be that these men were fully informed of our enterprise before they left Spain.

About daybreak they commenced to drift toward our ships; but our men, not having much faith in them, had during the night put up the sails so that they could be quickly cut down and be caught by the wind for a swift departure. Perceiving that this movement toward them by the Spaniards was not to do them any good, and well knowing that their facilities were inadequate to capture the Spaniards because most of the French were on shore, our men cut cables, abandoned their anchors, and sailed away.

The Spaniards, upon observing that they were discovered, let go some cannon volleys and set sail after the French, pursuing them all day long; but our men outdistanced them in the open sea. Then the Spaniards, apparently thinking that they could not capture our ships because our ships were better equipped in sails, and not wanting to leave the coast, pulled back and went on shore at the Seloy River, which we had named the River of Dolphins.[99] It was some eight or ten leagues from our place.

Our men, realizing their advantage in sails, followed the Spaniards to discover what they were doing. At dawn they returned to the River of May, where Captain Ribault, having seen them, went by barque to learn the news. At the entrance of the river he met the barque from Captain Cousette's ship. There were a good number of men in it and they told him of all the doings of the Spanish and how the great ship *Trinité* had taken to sea and had not yet returned. They also told him that they had seen three of the Spanish ships go into the River of Dolphins, that three others were at the roadstead there, and that the Spanish had put their infantry on land together with their foodstuffs and munitions. After receiving this news, Ribault returned to the fortress and came to my room where I was sick. There, in the presence of Captains la Grange, Saincte Marie, d'Ottigni, Visty, Yonville, and other gentlemen, he said that he felt it was necessary for the king's service that he embark with all of his forces and with the three ships that were in the road-stead in order to pursue the Spanish fleet. He asked our advices on this. I spoke first and cautioned against the consequences of such a project, telling him, among other things, about the dangerous winds that rise up on this coast, that if he should be driven on shore it would be very difficult to get to sea again, and that in the meantime those who stayed at the fort would be in danger and peril. Captains Saincte Marie and la Grange told him that they thought that it would not be wise to put any such project into effect and that it would be much better to hold the ground and fortify it; and that when the *Trinité*, which was the principal ship of all the vessels, had returned there would be a much better chance for success in such an enterprise.

Nevertheless, Captain Ribault resolved to undertake the effort, particularly since he had been informed by King Emola, one of our neighbors arriving during these consultations, that the Spaniards had gone ashore in great numbers and had seized the houses of Seloy and used them for their Negroes, whom they had brought to do labor. He said that they had now lodged themselves on the land and had made protective trenches around themselves. Because of the conclusions that Ribault had already arrived at and his believing, as he might well do, that the Spanish were camping there to attack us and to put us out of the land, he stood resolute and persistent in his embarking plans. He issued an order that all soldiers under his charge should embark with their arms and that his two ensigns should put everything under way. This was done.

He came to my room and asked me to lend him my lieutenant, my ensign, and my sergeant and to allow all my able soldiers to go with him. I refused him this, since, being sick myself, there was no one to handle the fort; and he responded that I need not doubt that he would return the next day and that in the meantime Lord du Lys would stay behind to take care of everything. I told him that since he was commander in this country, I did not have authority to deny him and that he should take good advice on what he did, lest something go astray. Then he told me that he could do nothing but continue his enterprise, because in a letter which he had received from the admiral there was a postscript, which he showed to me, written in these words, "Captain Jean Ribault, as I was closing up this letter I received advice that Don Pedro Menéndez has departed from Spain to go to the coast of New France. See that he does not encroach upon us any more than he would want you to encroach upon them." Ribault said to me, "Do you see the charge that I have, and I leave it to you to judge if you could do any less in this case, considering the definite advice that we have that they are landed and plan to invade us." This closed my mouth.

Thus having decided, or rather prejudged, this enterprise, and having more regard for his own opinion than for the advice that I had given him or for the trickiness of the weather, of which I had advised him, he embarked on September 8, taking with him thirty-eight of my men, together with my ensign. I speak now to those who know of warfare as to whether when an ensign marches, any soldier of spirit will stay behind and forsake his ensign. So no one remained with me in field command, because everyone followed him as the governor in whose name all proclamations and orders were given. Captain la Grange did not look favorably on this enterprise and stayed with me until the tenth of the month, and would not have gone then if it had not been for the strong requests made by Captain Ribault, who stayed two days at the roadstead waiting for Captain la Grange to join him. This being done, they sailed together, and I never saw them again.[100]

On September 10, the day they departed, such a great storm came up, with such heavy winds, that the Indians assured me that it was the worst that had ever come to that coast. Two or three days afterwards, believing that our ships were in peril, I sent for Lord du Lys to order assembled all of the remaining men and to advise them of the urgent need we had to repair our fortifications. I explained to them the dangers into which we might fall because of the absence of our ships and the proximity of the Spanish from whom we could expect an open and declared war, since they had landed and fortified themselves so close to us. I advised that if misfortune had come to those who were at sea, we might expect bad times since we were in such small numbers and in so many ways disabled. So everyone promised me to work.

Considering that our ration of food was very small and, if it were kept on that level, they would not be able to do much work, I increased the ration, even though since the arrival of Captain Ribault I had never taken any more food than an ordinary soldier and no longer had the means of giving even a bottle of wine as a reward to a soldier who seemed to deserve it. I was scarcely able to do this since the captain took with him two of my barques on which the remainder of the meal was stored, together with the biscuits which I had baked for our return to France. So, when I say that I received more generosity from the English strangers than from those from my own country, I am telling the truth.

We began to repair and refortify what had been demolished, principally on the river bank where I ordered sixty feet of timber to be replaced in order to re-establish the palisades. The planks for this came from the ship which I had built. Nothwithstanding all our diligence and work, it was not possible to rebuild the fort completely because of the bad weather and the winds.

Perceiving the great extremity of the situation, I reviewed the men left to me by Captain Ribault to see how many of them could bear arms. I found nine or ten, but I believe that no more than two or three had ever drawn a sword. Among those who say that there were sufficient persons to defend the fort, they should listen, and observe the men who were there. Of the nine, four were youths who served Captain Ribault in taking care of his dogs. The fifth was his cook. Among those who were outside the fort and who were in Captain Ribault's group there was a carpenter of at least sixty years of age,[101] a beermaker, an old crossbow maker, two shoemakers, four or five men with their wives, a spinet player, two servants of Lord du Lys, one of Beauhaire, one of Lord de la Grange, and about eighty-five or eighty-six laborers and women and children. This was the military force which was left to fight there. For my part, I leave it to others to consider if they were such able combatants why Captain Ribault would have traded them for the soldiers of mine whom he took in place of them.

Of those who remained from my company there were sixteen or seventeen who could bear arms, but they were all convalescent and sick. The rest were wounded and crippled persons, recovering from the battle which my lieutenant had made against Outina.

This review having been made, we formed our guard. We had two shifts so the soldiers could have one night free. Then, considering those most able among them, we selected two, one by the name of Lord de Sainct Cler, the other Lord de la Vigne, to whom we gave the lanterns and candles which were necessary in making the rounds because of the inclement weather. Then I lent them an hour glass so that the sentinels could serve equal shifts. I inspected the guard despite my sickness and the bad weather.

On the night between the nineteenth and the twentieth of September, La Vigne was in charge with his squad, and their duty was performed well in spite of the incessant rain. When day came and La Vigne saw that the weather was even worse than before, he took pity on the wet sentinels and, thinking that the Spanish would not come in such unusual weather, let the guard retire, and even he himself went to his lodgings. Meanwhile, someone who had something to do outside the fort, and my trumpeter, who was on one of the ramparts, saw a group of Spaniards coming down from a hill. They immediately sounded the alarm, including the trumpeter. When I heard this, I quickly ran out with my sword and with my round shield to protect me. Going to the middle of my fort, I called out to alert my soldiers. Some of the bravest of them went to the breach which was on the south side, and there they were repulsed and killed at the place where the artillery munitions were. Two battle flags came in by the same breach and were quickly set up. Two others entered through a breach on the west side. Our men who were lodged in that area came out from their beds and were killed.

As I went to give aid to those who were defending the breach on the side to the southwest, I was met there by a great number of Spaniards who had entered the fort by overcoming our men on that side. They drove me into the great court of the fortress, and there I saw Françqis Jean, one of the sailors who had stolen my boats in the mutiny. He had guided the Spaniards to this place. On seeing me, he began to shout that I was the captain of the fort. This group was led by a captain who was, in my opinion, Don Pedro Menéndez.

They struck me with their pikes, but I fended them off with my shield. Seeing that I could not overcome such a large company and that the fort was already taken, with their flags planted on the ramparts, and that I had no men still supporting me except one named Bartélemy, I went to the yard of my lodging, where they pursued me. If there had not been a tent there, I would have been taken. The Spaniards who followed me became involved in cutting the ropes of the tent, and as they did that I went through the breach on the west side near my lieutenant's lodgings and escaped into the woods. There I found a number of my men who had also escaped, of whom three or four were very seriously wounded.

I said to them: "Sons, since God has decided that this misfortune should come to us, what we should now do is to go as quickly as possible across the marshes and up to where our ships are at the mouth of the river." Some of them wanted to go to a little village which was in the woods, but the rest followed me through the reeds in the water. I had to stop because of my illness, and I then sent ahead two able swimmers to go to the ships to advise them of what had happened and to ask them to come help us.

They were unable to reach the ships that day, so I spent that night in water up to my shoulders, along with one of my men who would never leave me. The next morning I was scarcely able to draw breath; and I said my prayers to God, being joined in this by the soldier who remained with me, Jean du Chemin. I felt so weak that I believed I might die at any moment. Indeed, if this soldier had not gripped me so firmly in his arms in holding me out of the water, it would not have been possible for me to have survived.

After we had said our prayers, I heard a voice which seemed to me to come from one of those whom I had sent over by the ships to call for a small boat. This was the fact. The ships had been alerted concerning the events by Jean de Hais, my master carpenter, who had escaped by a barque. So they had sailed along the river bank to see if they could save anyone, and they did a good job of it. They went straight to the place where the two men were whom I had dispatched, and the two men called out to them. As soon as the men were taken aboard and had told them where I was, they set out to find me.

I was in very bad condition, and five or six of them carried me to the barque because I was not able to walk. When I came aboard the barque, the sailors took the shirts off their backs to cover me and wanted to take me promptly to the ships to give me some brandy. I insisted upon their first going among the reeds with their barque to search for any unfortunate companions who might be scattered around through there, and we recovered eighteen or twenty. The last one we recovered was the nephew of Treasurer le Beau.

After we had all come aboard the ships, I comforted them as much as I could and sent the barque back to see if they could pick up any more of our men. When they returned, the sailors told me that Captain Jacques Ribault,[102] who was in his ship about two gunshots distant from the fort, had spoken with the Spanish; and that François Jean had come to his ship, where he stayed a long time. The sailors were surprised that François Jean was allowed to depart from the ship, since it was he who brought about this event.

After I came aboard the ship *Levrier*, Captain Jacques Ribault and Captain Valuot came to see me, and we decided to return to France. Because I found this ship lacking captain, pilot, master, and boatswain's mate, I advised the selection of one from among the most capable of the sailors by their own choice. I took about six men and some equipment from a little ship which we finally had to sink because it lacked ballast and we could not sail her. Thus I increased the equipment of the ship in which I embarked, and I made master of the ship the one who had been boatswain's mate on the little ship we sunk. Since I lacked a pilot, I asked Jacques Ribault to let me have one of four men I named on his ship to act as my pilot. He promised to send them to me. Yet he did not do it when we were ready to sail, even though I told him that the thing I asked was for the service of the king.

I abandoned the ship which I had bought from the English captain, since I did not have the personnel to man it. Moreover, its equipment had been taken by Captain Jacques Ribault. I took from it only the artillery, which was all dismounted. Of this, I lent nine pieces to Jacques Ribault to carry back to France, and put five others into my own ship.

On September 25 we set sail to return to France. Captain Jacques Ribault and I sailed close together all that day and the next day until three or four o'clock in the afternoon. But since his bow was better than ours, he used the wind to better advantage and left us that day. We remained on our course and experienced some very high winds.

About October 28 at daybreak we saw the Isle of Flores in the Azores. As we approached the land, we experienced a great force of wind from the northwest, which kept us there for four days. Then the wind was from the south and southeast and was very fitful. During the passage we had nothing to eat but biscuits and water.

About November 10 or 11, after we had sailed a long time and were expecting that we were not far from land, I had my men take soundings and found seventy-five fathoms of water. This made us very happy. We thanked God for giving us such a good voyage.

Immediately after that we set sail again and continued our journey; but because we were blown too much toward the northwest we entered Saint George's Channel, a place feared by all navigators and where many have been shipwrecked. Nevertheless, God in His good grace allowed us to enter in good weather.

We navigated all night, hoping to be out of the mouth and to be at Dieppe the next morning. But we were frustrated in our efforts, for two or three hours after midnight, as I walked on the deck, I discovered land all about us, which was surprising. Immediately I ordered sails to be struck and the water sounded. We found that we had under us but eight fathoms of water, so I ordered remaining there until daybreak. This having arrived and my sailors not recognizing the land, I told them to go near shore.

There, near the land, I had the anchor dropped again and sent out a little boat to land men to determine in what country we were. They reported that we were in Wales, a province of England. I landed speedily and scarcely had taken a breath there when I became so ill that I thought I would die.

In the meantime I had this ship brought to the harbor, a little town called Swansey, where I found merchants of Saint Malo who lent me money to buy clothes for myself and for some of my company who were with me. Because there were no foodstuffs on the ship, I bought two beefs which I had salted, and a barrel of beer, which I gave to him in whose charge

I placed the ship, telling him to sail to France. This he promised to do. For my own part, I planned to go by land with my men. After saying goodbye to my sailors, I went by Swansey. There I slept with my companions at a place called Morgan. But the lord of the place, knowing of me, kept me with him for six or seven days. On my departure he was moved on account of my weakness and his generosity to give me a little carriage.

From there I went to Bristol and thence to London, where I paid my respects to Mr. de Foix, who is the ambassador for the king there. He took care of my money needs on account of my situation. From there I went to Calais and then to Paris. I was there advised that the king had gone to Moulins for a sojourn, to which place I went as quickly as I could, with a part of my company.[103]

This, in brief, is the story of all that happened in New France since it pleased the king to send his subjects there to explore the land. Objective and clearthinking readers can easily judge the merit of what was done and be competent critics of what I did there. For my part I will neither accuse nor excuse. It is enough for me to follow the truth of history, to which many can give witness, those who were actually present.

I will, however, plainly say that the long delay in the starting of the voyage of Captain Jean Ribault and the fifteen days that he sailed along the coast of Florida coming to La Caroline were the cause of the loss of Florida. He discovered the coast on August 14 and spent time going from river to river, sufficient time for unloading his ships and for me to embark for

France. I know full well that all of this was well intentioned. Nevertheless, it seems to me that he should have given more attention to his duties than to the inventions of his spirit, which sometimes were so deeply written in him that nothing could erase them. In this case it was a tragedy, because he had no sooner left us than a storm seized him and shipwrecked him on the coast. There, with all his vessels lost and scarcely saving himself from the waves, he fell into the hands of those who killed him, him and all of his company.

Appendix A

Newly Discovered Portrait of Dominique de Gourgues

René Laudonnière's account of his experience in Florida has customarily been published with an addition, not from his pen and about the voyage of Dominique de Gourgues and the French vengeance the latter imposed upon the Spanish in 1568. The story of that voyage was recently published in *Settlement of Florida* (Gainesville, University of Florida Press, 1968); and to add emphasis to it not being from Laudonniére's pen, it is not included here.

Nevertheless, as this volume goes to press, the author has been favored with permission to publish a reproduction of a portrait owned by relatives of Gourgues, and firmly believed by them to be his only authentic portrait. So it is published here.

A letter from the Baron de Bony, La Fontaine, Les Ormes, Vienne, France, dated October 22, 1971 says of the picture: "We are very honored that my ancestor's picture interests you. I do not know when that picture of Dominique de Gourgues was painted, but it has been in my family several centuries. It comes from the Castle of Vayus, near Bordeaux, which belonged to the Gourgues family many centuries. We are related to the Gourgues family through my father's mother, who was a Gourgues. That family name is now extinguished."

Appendix B

Laudonnière's Shipping Contract of 1572
By Jeannette Thurber Connor

When in 1964 the book Laudonnière and Fort Caroline *was published, it was believed that the original of René Laudonnière's 1572 shipping contract, mentioned at page 50 of that book, had been destroyed or lost; but since that time it has been found to be preserved in the Archives of the Département de la Charente-Maritime, at La Rochelle, France. The signature of Laudonnière on this contract reveals that it is identical with his 1573 signature which was reproduced at page 177 of the 1964 book.*

We are indebted to the late Mrs. Jeannette Thurber Connor for an interesting discussion of the contents of this contract and for a complete translation of it. These have been made available from the Connor papers in the Manuscript Division of the Library of Congress and follow herewith.

A curious document, discovered in La Rochelle by G. Musset, gives the information that in 1572, Laudonnière, who was both captain of the *Comtesse Testu,* and *"bourgeois* of the total of the said ship and furnishing a third part of all the merchandise," signed at La Rochelle one of those contracts called *tiercements,* which regulated at that period voyages beyond the seas. The vessel was to go to the "West Indies of Peru and other coasts and calling ports," where Captain René de Laudonnière and Master Guillaume Durant, "by the common opinion and advice of other officers and *tiercements*[1] . . . would consider it profitable to trade. . . ."

The contract belongs to a well-known class of deeds before notaries; Messrs. Ch. and P. Bréard have published several similar ones, the most ancient of which is nearly contemporaneous with Laudonnière's.[2]

The various parties mentioned in this particular deed are clearly defined: on the one hand, the Captain, who is at the same time the *bourgeois* (probably the owner) of the ship; on the other hand, the master, the *contremâitre* and a certain number of partners, called *tiercements;* and thirdly, the *masters victuallers.* The commercial aim of the voyage is just as clear: "to sell, barter and exchange" . . . until "the complete reloading of the said ship on the other side, to the best of their ability, for the profit of each one." The parties were to divide this profit on their return, according to custom: one third was to belong to the *bourgeois* of the vessel, that is to Laudonnière; a second, to the *victuallers;* a third, to the *tiercements* or shareholders. But "the beasts and birds shall be divided . . . half for the said *bourgeois* and *victuallers,* and the other half for the said *tiercements.*" Mr. G. Musset calls attention to this clause. For the *tiercements* to have thus asked for one-half instead of one-third, where the animals brought back by the expedition were concerned, they must have counted on these tropical "beasts and birds" being a great fad in France at that time. They undoubtedly hoped, Dr. E. T. Hamy observes in an article on Laudonnière,[3] thus to compensate themselves for all the trouble the capture and transportation of the animals had given them. Can one imagine what conditions must have existed on board that crowded small vessel, having as many as seventy men in the crew with delicate animals, accustomed to a southern climate, to be cared for and looked after!

Other interesting passages in the contract are to the effect that "the said *tiercements* have promised . . . for themselves and their crew, for whom in this respect they will be held responsible, not to board any ship, or plunder, or do any wrong or give any grievance to the friends, allies, and subjects of the king, our sovereign lord;" and have no other intention than "that the said ship shall be engaged in good and honest traffic."

The *Comtesse Testu* was in the road on May 16, 1572; she probably hoisted anchor a short time afterwards. Laudonnière's latest venture was going to save his life, says Dr. Hamy at the close of the article, for he was one of Coligny's familiars, he resided in Paris when he was not on the sea, and had he been in France that following fateful month of August, he would certainly have perished at the Admiral's side in the Saint Bartholomew Massacre.[4]

This is all that has been found out concerning the voyage to the "West Indies of Peru."

The Contract

Be it known, that before Vincent Naudin and Estienne Paillu, notaries and royal scribes in the city and government of La Rochelle, were present and personally identified Guillaume Durant, residing in Havre de Grâce, master of the ship called the *Comtesse Testue,* of one hundred and twenty tons or thereabouts, lying at present in the roadstead of Chef de Bois,[5] near this city aforesaid; Marin Harel, chief boatswain, Nycollas Nepveu, Jehan Collas, Estienne Letur, Mathieu Vyet, Jehan de Paris, Nycollas Rousselin, Samson Berthon, Guillaume de Caudebec, Jehan Drouet, Pierre Laudoneze, Rolland Berthe, all of them shareholders[6] of the said ship, and having a sharehold interest in the said ship for others as well as for themselves: Who, at their pleasure and of their free will, have acknowledged and declared, and do acknowledge and declare, that they have taken the aforesaid ship in thirds with the noble gentleman René de Laudonnière, captain of the said ship, residing in Paris, owner of the whole of the said ship, and furnishing one-third part of all the merchandise which has been furnished, loaded, and placed on board the said ship to go, with God's help, on the voyage hereafter declared; and [in thirds] with the noble Jehan de la Fons, lieutenant of Monsieur Sarrelabouz, knight of the Order of the King, our lord; and governor for his Majesty in the French city of [Havre] de Grâce; and with the honorable men Georges Fautrel, Jehan Faulcon, Toussainct, and Rolland called Berthes, merchants of Rouen; and with Jehan de Villette, instead of, and representing the right of the noble man Regnault de Marsollier, captain of a French company of infantry, at present in garrison at Calais; Raymond Aymerie, a Gascon merchant; of the aforesaid Masters Victuallers, the said sieurs de la Fons and Fautrel, for one quarter; de Villette,

Appendix B—Connor **175**

instead of the said Marsollier and Faulcon, each for half a quarter, Berthes, Aymerie, and the said master, the four of them, each for one-sixteenth;[7] the said Fautrel, de Villette, of the said name, and de la Fons and Raymond Aymerie, being absent, for whom the said Toussaintz Berthe stipulates by promise to recover it without loss; the said victuallers furnishing another third part of the goods, even the other third and last part in advance for the third of the said shareholders.

In order, God willing, to sail in the first seasonable weather from the said place and road of Chef de Bois, to go and take the said ship, and conduct her, pursuing a direct course, on the voyage to be made to the West Indies of Peru[8] and other coasts and ports of call where the said captain and master, by the common opinion and advice of the other officers and shareholders above-named, shall deem it profitable to carry on traffic with their said merchandise, according to the clearance given and forwarded for so doing; and in the above-said places, coasts, and ports of call, and at each of these, if they find it possible, to sell, barter, and exchange all and every of the said goods which they have acknowledged to have been duly furnished, given and delivered to them on board the said ship, for which they hold themselves accountable; and in exchange for the abovesaid, [to take on] other new merchandise, beasts, birds, and other things they may collect in those coasts and countries, which shall be good and suitable on this side [of the ocean], until the entire sale and distribution of the goods, and the complete reloading of the said ship there, to the best of their ability, for the profit of each one. The total cost of which goods, thus loaded, and the general average[9] thereon, has been found to amount, in conformity with the account and statement of this venture, to the sum of five thousand one hundred and ninety two livres, fourteen solz;[10] which, for the third of the said shareholders which, as has been said, the victuallers had advanced for them, and at their request, would amount to the sum of seventeen hundred and thirty-seven livres and eighteen solz *tournois;*[11] which loan, because the said shareholders said they had not the means to reimburse, and pay cash to, these victuallers [has been made] at the rate of forty-two livres, ten solz *tournois* per cent,[12] on account of the perils, risks, and adventures of the said victuallers with the said ship, either by sea or by war, as long as the said voyage shall last. Which sum of seventeen hundred and thirty livres and eighteen solz *tournois,* with the profit, at the abovesaid price, the said shareholders have consented, and obligated themselves, to give back and pay to the said victuallers, on the return of the said ship from this voyage, before they can take or remove any thing belonging to their said third on the return aforesaid. Which return shall be made, with God's help, to this harbor or any other under the King's rule, where God shall permit, allowing for the said perils and dangers of war and sea during the aforesaid voyage. At which said return, each and all of the said new goods, of whatever quality, species, and kind they be, proceeding from and being brought back from the said voyage, shall be divided at, and removed from, the place of the said landing, as above in the presence of the said owner, victuallers, and shareholders, or of persons acting for them, and not otherwise; and this by thirds, to wit: one third for the said owner of the said ship, another third for all the said victuallers, and the last for all the shareholders; except the beasts and birds, which shall be divided, in the presence of the above, half for the said owner and victuallers, and the other half for the said shareholders. Under penalty for those who shall be found to have hidden, removed, concealed, withheld, or otherwise diverted from the said general return, otherwise than in the presence of the above, of being charged with, convicted of, and punished for larceny, and of losing all that might belong to them for having made the said voyage. Likewise, neither the said shareholders nor any of their crew shall be able to make, beyond the seas, any sale or distribution of articles brought by them[13] before all the said merchandise has been traded and sold, under penalty of confiscation of the said articles and that proceeding there from; even of the interest, if the case call for it. And for the bonus and *chausses* of the said captain, the sum of thirteen hundred livres *tournois* has promised and granted to him by the above, both for him and for the masters and other officers of the said ship to whom a bonus may belong for having made the said voyage, as is the custom;

Laudonnière's signature on a 1572 shipping contract.

on condition that the said captain, master, and Berthes, the clerk, have duly consented and obligated themselves to make out the invoice of the said merchandise, draw up and adjust the statement and tally, and prove on their said return, as is requisite and necessary in such case; without any other payment being made to them for this than the above bonus. And these above shareholders have promised to make up their crew of seventy men capable to make the said voyage, the said captain, shareholders and pages[14] included; the wages of those who are to be paid, these shareholders shall be bound to pay and satisfy from the revenue of their said third, on the return from the said voyage, and to relieve the said owner and victuallers from trouble and inconvenience therein. Furthermore, these shareholders have promised on the said return, to give preference to the said victuallers above all others in the purchase of the said goods which shall proceed from their said third, at the price which, without fraud, would be offered them by others. The aforesaid owner, victuallers, and shareholders declaring and stipulating respectively, as is said, that the said ship is well and duly repaired, caulked, rigged, furnished with all things necessary, duly victualled and provided with good, proper and suitable merchandise, and in sufficient quantity, wherein they have held and do hold themselves to be well satisfied.

And in consequence, the said parties promised and swore, as in fact they have promised and sworn, each of his own free will, to hold and guard the contents of the present contract inviolably, without infringing, under penalty of all costs, damages and interest; under the pledge and mortgage of each and all of their property, present and to come. And besides the above, the said shareholders have promised, and shall be held thereto, for themselves and their crew, for whom in this respect they shall be held responsible, not to board any ship, or plunder, or do any wrong or harm to the friends, allies, and subjects of the King, our sovereign lord; rather shall they give them aid and comfort, if they be in need therof and request it; and they shall keep and observe inviolably the orders of the King our said lord, in the matter of navigation, and the contents of the said clearance granted and forwarded to them for the said voyage, without in any way contravening it. Likewise, each one shall give obedience to the said captain, navigators and officers of the said ship, to each according to his rank, so that all may be conducted in good order, without confusion; under penalty, for the delinquents and transgressors, of being accused, convicted, and punished as infringers of the King's ordinances and rebels to his Majesty, and of being held responsible for all interest to the said owner and victuallers, as shall be fitting. And in case of infringement in what is said, the said owner and victuallers have disclaimed and denied, and do disclaim and deny, at the present time and henceforth, that they are in any way answerable therefor; they protest that they are not; relying on it that the law will see that punishment be given to the delinquents, as shall be fitting; because it is their intention, which they have now declared, that the said ship goes for honest and loyal traffic.

Wherefore, for the fulfilment of the above, as is written, the said parties of their own consent and free-will have wished to be sworn before the said notaries.

La Rochelle, the XVI of May, in the year one thousand five hundred and seventy-two.

Appendix C

Mutual Gift Agreement between René Laudonnière and His Wife

The Honorable M. Delafosse, Director in Chief of the Archives of Seine-et-Oise at Versailles, France, has recently discovered in those archives a donation agreement between René Laudonnière and his wife Geneviefve (Genevieve) Maillard. He generously transcribed the difficult and ancient handwriting into legible French and allowed its first publication in this volume. Miss Salomé Mandel, of Paris, who also generously helped in the production of this volume, brought this discovery to the author's attention, suggesting its inclusion.

This is the first proof available to modern historians that Laudonnière was ever married. It reveals a long standing marriage, in a tender and affectionate relationship. Rather than being a signed contract it is a formal announcement before a notary of an agreement that the couple's mutual properties, real and personal, would be held by the survivor of them to the exclusion of the heirs of either of them.

The original document, executed at Saint-Germain-en-Laye, is partially incomplete, as some of its words have been obliterated with the passage of time. However, a copy has also been found, one which was filed contemporaneously in the city hall at Paris; and it is complete. The Paris copy, dated September 13, 1572, is in the Archives Nationales, under the file notation of Folio 221, y113. It is preceded by the following words, here translated into English, which words are not in the original:

"Registration in the records of the City Hall of Paris, concerning the donation: Laudonnière-Maillard"

"Greetings to all those who inspect these papers, from Richard Comberel, agent for the King, his lord in the provostship of Saint-Germain-en-Laye, and his Majesty's guardian of the seals of said place. Be informed that before François Fremont, notary and royal keeper of the records at said Saint-Germain, there came personally René de Laudonnière, Esquire, gentleman of said place and captain in the employment of the King, and Madame Geneviefve Maillard, his wife, by whom the said notary was sufficiently authorized to make and report the following."

The text of the donation, translated into English from the original document as amplified by the Paris copy, reads as follows:

"Series E. Minutes of Fremont, notary at Saint-Germain-en-Laye, between the 10th and 14th of September, 1572"

"Mutual Gift Between Laudonnière and His Wife"

"Laudonnière and Maillard, being prosperous and of good health in mind and body and having so declared themselves and it so appearing to the undersigned notary; they, considering the many great kindnesses, affectionate sharings, attentions and services that they have enjoyed between them during and steadfastly throughout their marriage, constantly day in and day out; and still hoping for this to continue, even better and better, as God may grant for as long as they shall live together in marriage; and considering also the great effort, careful labor and industry that each of them has put forth and endured to acquire and preserve such personal properties and lands as our Lord Jesus Christ has graciously allowed them to enjoy during their mortal life; and they, wishing with all their hearts and beings to recompense one another—as much as they might wish it to be more—and more adequately to manage and maintain their estate:

"For these reasons and others that prompt them to this course, Laudonnière and Maillard, having spoken of their own free wills, completely voluntarily acting on accurate information, without coercion, fraud, or constraint and upon good counsel given freely and deliberately; and having made their statements by verification and acknowledgment in the presence of and before the said notary; they did make a fitting determination which is repeated here by the terms of these presents, witnessing a mutual agreement disposing equally of all the said personal and real property which they have acquired and will acquire during their marriage, and which they will hold in common together at the day and hour of the death of the first of them to die.

"By virtue of this mutual donation and equal gift, the said Laudonnière and Maillard desire and expressly agree that the survivor and last of them to die shall hold, fully possess and peacefully use during his or her lifetime in whatever state of being or condition, without any constraint or obstruction whatsoever, every part and parcel of said first decedent's personal property, trust revenues and real property, and without the surviving and last decedent having to give any bond whatsoever to the heirs of the first decedent for the delivering of such property, other than surety under oath; saving and reserving however for the first decedent his or her part and portion of such personal and real property under individual control and reserving such quantity of property and money as shall appear necessary to carry out his or her last will and testament, which said donation and equal gift Laudonnière and Maillard, and each of them, wish to be accomplished, and so give their clear and complete consent, force and approval according to the terms and text;

"And neither Laudonnière nor Maillard can revoke or retract this donation and mutual gift without the consent of the other.

"And said Laudonnière and Maillard desire and will that their heirs, each in his own regard, should be constrained to hold and protect this mutual donation and equal gift, without making or giving any interference, impeachment, repudiation or overruling; and said married couple disinherit from now to then and from then to now, those heirs who try to come against this mutual gift and donation of goods and property and those who have the daring to impeach the intent of these presents.

"For registration in the record office of the City Hall at Paris and every other appropriate place, and appointing as agent to do this the Sieur de Laudonnière; Master Charles Audray, agent at St. Germain-en-Laye; the said Geneviefve Maillard; Master Michel Paramour, also agent at said place; to whom, and to each of them respectively, these parties have given and are giving full power, strength and authority to do this and everything that will concern and be necessary to it, pursuant to the orders of the King; for it has been so stated, convened and expressly agreed to between the said parties.

"Promising, etc., obliging, etc., relinquishing, etc. Done and approved at said Saint-Germain-en-Laye in the presence of the Honorable Sirs: Jehan Chalveau, Master of the King's Buildings and Grounds at said Saint-Germain-en-Laye; Claude Nepveu, Master Glazier, in the glass works of the said place; Nicolas Domaille and other witnesses."

Appendix D

Plant Life in Sixteenth-Century Florida
By Tom V. Wilder

In 1959 the National Park Service asked the Library of Congress to identify plant life that would have been present and used by the French at Fort Caroline or among the neighboring sixteenth-century Indians. The purpose of the study was to provide the information necessary for a project to replant and protect native plants as a part of the outdoor exhibits of the Fort Caroline National Memorial. The project has not yet been carried out, but the Garden Club of Jacksonville has volunteered to assist in such a program; and it is expected to be undertaken sometime in the near future.

Tom Wilder of the Natural Resources Division of the Library of Congress wrote the paper which had been requested; and it is first published herewith.

Laudonnière, in writing of the hill lying behind the then existing (1564) expanse of low-lying ground on which he chose to erect Fort Caroline, referred to the height of what is now known as St. Johns Bluff. Apparently no site seemed more suited for his settlement than the ground area lying between the Bluff and the river, an area which in his time was reported as being highly cultivated by the Indians with fields of mil, maize, beans, and pumpkins.

Writing of the hill, Laudonnière states, according to Hakluyt's translation (René Laudonnière, *A Notable History* [Farnham, Eng.: Henry Stevens, Son & Stiles, 1964], p. 22) as follows:

> Nowe was I determined to search out the qualities of the hill. Therefore I went right to the toppe thereof, where we found nothing else but Cedars, Palme, and Baytrees of so souereigne odour, that Baulme smelleth nothing like in comparison. The trees were environed rounde about with Vines bearing grapes in such quantitie, that the number would suffice to make the place habitable. Besides this fertilitie of the soyle for Vines, a man may see Esquine wreathed about the shrubs in great quantitie. Touching the pleasure of the place, the Sea may bee seene plaine and open from it, and more than sixe great leagues off, neere the Riuer Belle, a man may beholde the medowes divided asunder into Iles and Islets enterlacing one another: Briefly the place is so pleasant, that those which are melancholicke would be inforced to change their humour.

The sixteenth-century drawings of Fort Caroline made by LeMoyne indicate that the uncultivated area on which the fort was built was covered with a substantial growth of what appears to have been *Juniperus barbadensis*, scattered clumps of Sabal Palmettos and *Persea borbonia* (Laurel, Sweetbay, Red Bay), with an understory of Yucca, presumably *Yucca aloifolia*, since some Yucca are shown as flowering at the time of construction. Also what appears to be a solitary live oak is depicted with a heavy covering of *Dendropogon usneoides* (Spanish Moss). See Charles E. Bennett, compiler, *Settlement of Florida* (Gainesville: University of Florida Press, 1968), p. 1.

PLANT SOURCES OF FOODS USED OR AVAILABLE

TO TIMUCUANS

"All the tribes of North American Indians supplemented their common fare of fish and game with fruits and vegetables. Corn, beans, pumpkins, and squashes grew so well that their culture, in some tribes, such as the Cherokees and Iroquis, furnished the chief means of sustenance. These four vegetables along with tobacco, gourds, and the sunflower, came to our Northern Indians from Peru by way of Mexico." (H. P. Hedrick, *A History of Horticulture in America to 1860* [N.Y., Oxford University Press, 1950]), p. 3.

"Before Columbus came to the New World, South American food plants had been carried North and East as far as Canada and New England" (Ibid., p. 3–4).

"More than two hundred species of tree, bush, vine, and small fruits were in common use by Indians when whites came. Besides these there were at least 50 varieties of nuts, and even greater number of herbaceous plants. Although but few bulbs were cultivated, wild bulbs were eaten by the Indians in time of famine" (Ibid., p. 4).

"Yet the botanical knowledge of early North American Indians was not inconsiderable. They knew a half hundred or more plants that were good for food or drink; they used as many more for their physical ailments; perhaps quite as many more were collected for dyes, deodorants, hair tonics, and clothing" (Ibid., p. 4).

"Beans, corn, pumpkins and squash were the four sisters of Indian agriculture, where one was grown, the others were almost always found in the same field" (Ibid., p. 12).

One of the difficulties in stating with certainty that specific plants were or were not used or available to the Timucuans is the matter of European and South American introductions. For example, European-origin peas were reported by Cartier to be grown by the Indians near Montreal in 1535. Similarly, Laudonnière, writing of Ribault's first voyage, relates in 1562 that peas were cultivated by the Timucuans, presumably as distinguished from beans. Laudonnière also relates that upon going ashore near the mouth of the River of May, he found a "great store of Mulberrie trees white and red, on the toppes whereof there was an infinite number of silke wormes." This despite the fact that the white mulberry is authoritatively reported as being introduced and naturalized from Asia (M. L. Fernald, *Gray's Manual of Botany* [New York: American Book Co., 1950]).

The writings of Laudonnière and the illustrations and descriptions of Le Moyne respecting the Timucuans specifically identify a number of plant sources of food. And others were undoubtedly used, because they were available to the Eastern Timucuans and were authoritatively reported by others. In addition to the staple items of peas, beans, squash, pumpkins, and maize, the following plant sources of food were used, or believed known to the Timucuans.

PLANT	PARTS USED	USE
Acer floridanum (Southern Sugar Maple)	Sap	Syrup and sugar
Acer rubrum trilobum (Trident Red Maple)	Sap	Syrup and sugar
Aesculus pavia (Red Buckeye)	Nuts	Meal for breadstuff
Allium (Wild Onions, Garlic) A. *canadensis* A. *mutabile*	Bulbs	Vegetable
Amelanchier intermedia (Swamp Serviceberry)	Fruit	Fresh fruit and cooked or dried for winter use
Amphicarpa bracteata	Subterranean fruits	Beans
Apios americana (Ground Nut, Indian Potato, Potato-Bean)	Seeds Tuberous Rootstocks	Beans Vegetable

Plant	Parts Used	Used As
Arisaema dracontium (Dragon-Root, Indian Turnip)	Root	Breadstuff
Arundinaria (Cane)	Grain	Meal
	Shoots	Vegetable
A. tecta (Switch Cane)		
A. gigantea (Large Cane)		
Asclepias (Milkweed)	Young shoots	Cooked vegetable
A. viridiflora		
A. lanceolata		
A. rubra		
A. perennis		
A. variegata		
A. amplexicaulis		
A. longifolia		
Asclepiodora viridis (Spider Milkweed)	Young shoots	Cooked vegetable
Asimina triloba (North American Paw Paw)	Fruit	Fresh fruit and cooked
Callicarpa americana (French Mulberry)	Fruit	Fruit
Capsicum frutescens (Capsicum)	Fruit	Seasoning pepper
Cardamine pensylvanica (Native Water Cress)	Leaves and stems	Uncooked greens
Carya (Hickory)	Nuts	Nuts, dried, oil, cakes, meal, butter.
	Sap	Sugar, syrup.
C. ashei (Florida Pignut)		
C. glabra megacarpa		
C. tomentosa		
Castanea (Chestnut)	Nuts	Nuts, cooked vegetable, breadstuff, meal or flour.
C. dentata (Chestnut)		
C. pumila (Chinquapin)		
Ceanothus americanus intermedius (Redroot)	Leaves	Tea
Celtis (Hackberry)	Fruit	Fresh fruit
	Seeds	Condiment
C. occidentalis		
C. tenuifolia		
C. laevigata smallii		
Chenopodium berlandieri (Pigweed)	Seeds	Breadstuff, flour or meal
	Leaves and stems	Cooked greens
Clethra alnifolia (Sweet Pepperbush)	Leaves	Cooked vegetable
Crataegus (Hawthorn, Red-Haw)		
C. flava	Fruit	Cooked fruit
C. phaenopyrum		
C. spathulata		

188   *Three Voyages*

PLANT	PARTS USED	USED AS
C. viridis		
C. marshallii		
Cunila origanoides	Leaves	Herb
(Dittany)		
Diospyros virginiana	Fruit	Fresh fruit and
(Common Persimmon—Mespilorum		cooked, meal for
by Le Moyne—Medlars by		breadmaking, syrup
Laudonnière)		
Fagus grandifolia caroliniana	Nuts	Dried meal cakes,
(Beech)		nuts, meal or
(Beech not normally found in		flour, oil, bread
eastern part of northwestern		
part of north Florida but mast		
could have been available if		
desired by eastern Timucuans.)		
Gaylussacia (Huckleberry)	Fruit	Fresh fruit and
		also dried
G. dumosa (Dwarf Huckleberry)		
G. frondosa (Dangleberry)		
Glyceria striata	Grain	Flour
(Fowl Meadow Grass)		
Hedeoma pulegioides	Leaves	Pot herb
(Mock Pennyroyal)		
Helianthus (Sunflower)		

(While the large sunflowers appear in the earliest drawings illustrating the Indian plantings in the Virginia area, they do not appear in those made by Le Moyne of the Timucuans' cultivation. On this basis it might be concluded that the Timucuans did not make use of sunflower seeds to make flour for breadstuffs and oil.)

Hyptis mutabilis	Leaves	Pot herb
(Hyptis)		
Ilex (Holly)	Leaves	Tea
I. vomitoria (youpon, cassena)		
I. cassine (Cassine)		
I. glabra (Inkberry)		
Juglans nigra (Black Walnut)	Nuts	Nuts, oil, meal,
(Black walnut not normally		dried cakes, butter.
found in northeastern part	Sap	Syrup, sugar.
of north Florida, but nuts		
could have been available		
if desired by eastern		
Timucuans)		
Lactuca (Lettuce, Milkweed)	Leaves	Uncooked greens
L. floridana		and potherbs
L. floridana villosa		
Lilium (True Lilies)	Bulbs	Vegetable
L. catesbaci		
L. michauxii		
Lycopus (Water Horehound)	Roots	Relish and cooked
L. americanus		vegetable
L. rubellus		

Plant	Parts Used	Used As
L. amplectens		
Malus augustifolia	Fruit	Cooked fruit
(Narrow-leaved Crabapple		and cider
Southern Crabapple)		
Medeola virginiana	Roots	Uncooked with
(Indiana Cucumber Root)		salad greens
Melissa officinalis	Leaves	Potherb
(Balm)		
Mitchella repens	Fruit	Fresh fruit
(Two-eyed-berry, Running Box)		
Monarda punctata	Leaves	Potherb
(Horse Mint)		
Morus rubra (Red Mulberry)	Fruit	Fresh fruit and
		cooked
Morus alba (White Mulberry)		
Myrica (Wax-Myrtle)	Berries	Flavoring
M. *cerifera*	Leaves	Potherb
M. *pusilla*		
Nelumbo lutea	Rootstocks	Baked vegetable.
(Water Chinquapin)	Seeds	Nutlike fruit,
		cooked vegetable,
		meal
Nuphar advena	Roots, seeds	Vegetable, breadstuff.
(Spatter-Dock)	Roots	Vegetable, fresh
Nymphaea odorata-gigantea	Flower buds	Delicacy
(Fragrant Water Lily)		
Nyssa ogeche	Fruit	Fresh fruit and cooked,
(Ogeeche Lime or Plum)		acid drink
Opuntia incarnata (Indian Fig)	Fruit	Fresh fruit and cooked.
Orontium aquaticum	Roots	Baked vegetable.
(Golden Club)		
Passiflora incarnata	Fruit	Fresh fruit
(Maypop, Passionflower		
Apricot Vine)		
Peltandra virginica	Roots	Baked vegetable.
(Tuckahoe)	Seeds	Breadstuff
Persea borbonia	Leaves	Potherb
(Red Bay)		
Phaseolus polystachios	Seeds	Beans
(Kidney Bean)		
Physalis (Ground Cherry	Fruit	Fresh fruit and
Strawberry-Tomato)		cooked
P. *pubescens*		
P. *pruinosa*		
P. *angulata*		
P. *maritima*		
P. *virginiana*		
Physostegia (False Dragonhead)	Leaves	Potherb
P. *denticulata*		
P. *obovata*		
Phytolacca americana	Young leafy sprouts	Cooked greens
(Pokeweed)		

Plant	Parts Used	Used As
Podophyllum peltatum (May-Apple)	Fruit	Fresh fruit and cooked
Polygonum (Smartweed)	Leaves Seeds	Seasoning Flour meal
P. *scandens*		
P. *pensylvanicum durum*		
P. *punctatum*		
P. *robustius*		
P. *hydropiperoides*		
P. *opelousanum*		
P. *setaceum*		
P. *sagittatum*		
P. *artifolium*		
P. *cristatum*		
Pontederia (Pickerelweed)	Seeds Leaves and stems	Fresh, and dried Vegetable
P. *cordata*		
P. *lanceolata*		
Prunus (Cherry, Plum)	Fruit	Fresh fruit and/or cooked
P. *americana* (Wild Yellow Plum)		
P. *angustifolia* (Chicasaw Plum)		
P. *serotina* (Black Cherry)		
P. *umbellata* (Black Sloe)		
Pteridium pseudocaudatum (Broken Fern)	Young croziers	Vegetable
Pycnanthemum (Basil)	Leaves	Potherb
P. *setosum*		
P. *flexuosum*		
Quercus (Oak)	Nuts	Nuts, breadstuffs
Q. *alba* (White Oak)		
Q. *stellata* (Post Oak)		
Q. *lyrata* (Overcup Oak)		
Q. *prinus* (Swamp Chestnut Oak)		
Q. *muhlenbergii* (Chinkapin Oak)		
Q. *velutina* (Black Oak)		
Q. *laevis* (Turkey Oak)		
Q. *nigra* (Water Oak)		
Q. *phellos* (Willow Oak)		
Q. *laurifolia* (Laurel Oak)		
Q. *cinerea* (Upland Willow Oak)		
Q. *virginiana* (Live Oak)		
Rhamnus caroliniana (Indian Cherry)	Fruit	Fresh fruit and cooked
Rhexia (Deergrass)	Leaves	Uncooked greens
R. *ciliosa*		
R. *virginica* var. *septemnervia*		
R. *mariana*		
Rhus copallina (Dwarf Sumac)	Fruit	Fresh fruit, acid drink
	Beans	Dried for drink making in winter

Appendix D—Wilder   191

PLANT	PARTS USED	USED AS
Rubus (Black Raspberry, Southern Dewberry) *R. occidentalis* (Black Raspberry) *R. triviales* (Southern Dewberry)	Fruit	Fresh fruit and cooked
Rumex (Docks, Sorrell) *R. verticillatus* *R. pulcher*	Leaves and stems	Cooked greens
Sabal palmetto (Cabbage Palmetto)	Terminal buds Fruit	Cooked vegetable Fresh fruit
Sagittaria (Swamp Potato) *S. subulata* var. *natans* *S. falcata*	Root tubers	Vegetable
Salvia (Sage) *S. lyrata* *S. urticifolia*	Leaves	Potherb
Sassafras albidum var. *molle* (Sassafras)	Leaves	Dried and powdered for flavoring.
	Root	Tea
Scirpus etuberculatus (Tall-Bulrush, "Tule")	Roots Young roots Seeds Tips of new growth in fall	Breadstuff Syrup Vegetable Vegetable
Scutellaria integrifolia var. *hispida* (Skullcap)	Leaves	Potherb
Serenoa serrulata (Saw Palmetto)	Fruit	Fresh fruit
Sesuvium maritimum (Sea-Purslane)	Leaves	Cooked greens
Sium (Water Parsnip) *S. suave* *S. floridanum*	Root Leaves	Vegetable Relish
Smilax (Greenbrier) *S. tamnoides* (China-Root) *S. glauca* (Sawbrier) *S. bona-nox*	Tuberous rootstocks	Reddish flour or meal used in soups and breadmaking, also with cooked fruits.
Stellaria pubera (Chickweed)	Growing tips	Cooked greens
Strophostyles (Groundnut–Wild Bean) *S. helvola* *S. umbellata*	Roots Seeds	Cooked vegetable Beans
Suaeda linearis (Sea Blight)	Young branches and leaves	Cooked greens
Teucrium canadense (Wood Sage)	Leaves	Potherb
Tradescantia rosea graminea (Spiderwort)	Roots and leaves	Vegetable

PLANT	PARTS USED	USED AS
Trianthema portulacastrum (Sea-Purslane)	Leaves	Cooked greens
Uvularia perfoliata (Wild Oats)	Roots and Young shoots	Vegetable
Vaccinium (Blueberry-Sparkleberry) *V. arboreum* (Sparkleberry) *V. elliottii* (Blueberry) *V. tenellum* (Dwarf—Low Bush Blueberry) *V. caesariense* (High Bush Blueberry) *V. atrococcum* (Black High Bush Blueberry) *V. stamineum* (Deerberry)	Fruit	Fresh fruit and cooked—also dried
Valerianella radiata (Corn Salad)	Leaves and Stems	Uncooked greens
Viola esculenta (Violet)	Leaves and flowers	Potherb
Vitis (Grape) *V. cinerea* var. *floridana* (pigeon grape) *V. vulpina* (winter grape) *V. rotundifolia* (muscadine grape)	Fruit	Fresh fruit and cooked—also dried
Yucca aloifolia (Spanish Bayonet)	Fruit	Fresh fruit
Zamia integrifolia coontie *Z. silvicola* coontie *Z. umbrosa* coontie	Root	Breadstuff

(The use of the roots of this plant to make meal for bread is related by Laudonnière on page 406 of "Hakluyt's Early Voyages," vol. III. While these large representatives of prehistoric plants grow abundantly in the pinelands of South Florida–it does grow in sandy places in other parts of Florida. However, there is no apparent evidence that the Northeastern Timucuans traded for it or made use of it as did the Florida Indians further south. However, it was known to the French and their Timucuan associates by reputation.)

Zizaniopsis miliacea (Water-Millet)	Cane-shoots	Vegetable
	Grain	Meal

PLANT SOURCES OF MEDICINALS USED
OR AVAILABLE TO THE TIMUCUANS

The description of Jacques Le Moyne's drawing dealing with the Timucuan mode of treating the sick is not specific as to the medicaments used except with respect to "topaco" meaning tobacco. This description as given on pages 8 and 9 of the "Descriptions of the Illustrations" drawn by Jacques Le Moyne in Florida in 1564, is:

> Their way of curing diseases is as follows: They put up a bench or platform of sufficient length and breadth for the patient, as seen in the

Appendix D—Wilder   193

plate, and lay the sick person upon it with his face up or down, according to the nature of his complaint; and, cutting into the skin of the forehead with a sharp shell, they suck out blood with their mouths, and spit it into an earthen vessel or a gourd bottle. Women who are suckling boys, or who are with child, come and drink this blood, particularly if it is that of a strong young man; as it is expected to make their milk better, and to render the children who have the benefit of it bolder and more energetic. For those who are laid on their faces, they prepare fumigations by throwing certain seeds on hot coals; the smoke being to pass through the nose and mouth into all parts of the body, and thus to act as a vomit, or to overcome and expel the cause of the disease. They have a certain plant whose name has escaped me, which the Brazilians call *petum*, and the Spaniards *topaco*. The leaves of this, carefully dried, they place in the wider part of a pipe; and setting them on fire, and putting the other end in their mouths, they inhale the smoke so strongly, that it comes out of their mouths and noses, and operates powerfully to expel the humors. In particular, they are extremely subject to the venereal disease, for curing which they have remedies of their own, supplied by nature."

Laudonnière relates generally in his description of Florida as follows:

They haue their Priests to whom they giue great credit, because they are great magicians, great soothsayers, and callers vpon diuels. These Priests serue tham instead of Physitions and Chirurgions. They carry always about them a bag full of herbes and drugs to cure the sicke diseased which for the most part are sicke of the pocks, (syphilus) for they loue women and maidens exceedingly, which they call the daughters of the Sunne: and some of them are Sodomites."
They have a custome among them, that when they find themselues sicke, where they feele the paine, whereas we cause our selues to be let blood, their Physitions sucke them vntill they make the blood follow. Esquine a drugge excellent against the pockes.

Although the French make little or no mention of the medicinal properties of sassafrass as such, Nicholas Monardes (Physician of Seville) in 1574 tells in his writings, entitled "Joyfull Newes Out of the Newe Founde Worlde," of its great medicinal value to the French at Fort Caroline and to the Spanish successors to that outpost prior to its destruction by Dominique de Gourgues. Monardes was first told of the virtues of sassafrass by a Frenchman, presumably a captive of the Spanish conquest of Fort Caroline. The Frenchman, according to Monardes, told him of the French grievous and various diseases, which due to the Indians showing them the sassafrass tree and the manner how they (the Indians) used it, were cured and healed by use of the water made from the tree. He relates the method of preparation learned from the Timucuans by the French and Spanish, its remarkable curative powers against the sicknesses of the Spanish soldiers lately returned from Florida, and the respective merits of the parts of the tree, as follows:

> Thei tooke up the roote of this Tree, and tooke a peece thereof, suche as it seemed to theim beste, thei cutte it small into verie thinne, and little peeces, and cast them into water, at discretion, that whiche thei sawe was needefull, little more or lesse, and thei sodde it the tyme that semed nedefull, for to remaine of a good coulour, and so thei dranke it, in the mornyng fastyng, and in the daie tyme, and at dinner and supper, without kepyng any more weight, or measure, then I have saied, nor more keepyng, nor order then this, and of this thei were healed of so many griefes, and evill deseases. That to heare of them what thei suffred, and how thei were healed, it doeth bryng admiration, and thei whiche were whole dranke it in place of wine, for it doeth preserve them in healthe: as it did appeare verie well by theim, that hath come from thence this yere. . . .
> . . . The Indians doeth use to put them beaten or stamped upon bruises, or of any manne beaten with drie blowes, and beeyng drie, thei are used in Medicinable thynges. . . .
> The beste of all the Tree is the roote, and that dooeth woorke the beste effecte, the whiche hath the rinde verie fast to the inner parte, and it is of the coulour Taunie, and muche more of swete smell then all the Tree, and his braunches, the rinde dooeth taste of a more sweete smell, then the Tree, and the water beeyng sodden with the roote, is of greater and better effectes, then of any other parte of the Tree. . . .

Plant sources of medicinal materials indigenous to the historic area of Fort Caroline and vicinity which from all indications were available to the Timucuans and used either alone or in combination by them and their successors, the Creeks, are as follows:

PLANT	PARTS USED	AILMENTS TREATED
Aesculas pavia	Roots	Dyspepsia
(Red Buckeye)	Chopped leaves and sprigs	Bath for smallpox prevention
Baptisia tinctoria	Roots	Emetic, cathartic
(False Indigo-Rattleweed)		
Eryngium yuccifolium	Roots	Neuralgia
(Button-Snakeroot)	Leaves	Dysentery
Eupatorium—(Thoroughwort)	Leaves	Emetic
E. fistulosum		
E. capillifolium		
E. album var. *glandulosum*		
E. leucolepis		
E. cuneifolium		
E. linearifolium		
E. recurvans		
E. hyssopifolium		
E. pilosum		
E. pubescens		
E. rotundifolium		

PLANT	PARTS USED	AILMENTS TREATED
Gnaphalium obtusifolium (Catfoot—Everlasting)	Leaves	Mumps
Ilex vomitoria (Cassina—Yaupon)	Leaves	Stimulant Emetic
Lindera benzoin pubescens (Wild Allspice or Fever Bush)	Branches	Emetic
Nicotiana rustica (Tapaco—Tabaco—Petum Wild Tobacco)	Leaves	"Expell the humors" as phlegm, melancholy, etc.
Parthenocissus quinquefolia (Virginia Creeper)	Roots	Gonorrhea
Platanus occidentalis (Sycamore)	Roots, bark	Tuberculosis
Populus heterophylla (Swamp Cottonwood)	Roots	Dysentery Nose Bleed Fevers
Prunus angustifolia (Chickasaw Plum)	Roots	Dysentery
Prunus scrotina (Black Cherry)	Inner bark	Dyspepsia Prunus
Quercus stellata (Post Oak)	Inner bark	Dysentery
Rhus copallina (Dwarf Sumac)	Root	Dysentery
Sassafras albidum var. *molle* (Sassafras—Pauame)	Roots, leaves and pith of twigs	Jaundice, kidney trouble, gall stones, fevers
Smilax (Esquine—Greenbrier—Catbrier)		
S. tamnoides (China-Root)	Roots	Syphilis
S. glauca (Wild sarsaparilla)	Roots	Syphilis
S. bona-nox var. *hastata* (China-Brier)	Roots	Syphilis Ulcers
Spigelia marilandica (Indian Pink)	Roots	Worm expellent
Stillingia sylvatica (Queens Delight)	Roots	Emetic, carthartic
Tephrosia Virginiana (Goats-rue, Rabbit's pea)	Roots	Bladder trouble

PLANT SOURCES OF DYES USED OR AVAILABLE TO THE TIMUCUANS

Although nothing specific with respect to particular plants in reference to the development of dye materials by the Timucuans appears in the writings of M. René Laudonnière and the writings and drawings of Jacques Le Moyne, it is generally clear that they have developed dyes of a number of colors primarily from vegetative sources. Laudonnière in his writings (pages 369 and 372 of "Hakluyt's Translation of accounts of Early Voyages," Vol. III) states:

". . . There is also in this Countrey a great store of graynes and herbes, whereof might be made excellent good dyes and paintings of all kind of colours. And in trueth the Indians which take pleasure in painting of their skins, know very well how to vse the same. . . ."

"The King gaue our Captaine at his departure a plume or fanne of Hernshawes feathers died in red, and a basket made of Palm-boughes after the Indian fashion, and wrought very artificially, and a great skinne painted and drawen throughout with the pictures of diuers wild beastes so liuely drawn and pourtrayed, that no thing lacked but life."

Plant sources of dye materials indigenous to the historic area of Fort Caroline and vicinity, which from all indications were available to the Timucuans and could have been used by them either separately or in many possible combinations to produce the various colors and effects they desired, are as follows:

PLANT	PARTS USED	COLORS OF DYES
Allium canadense (Wild Garlic)	Skins	Burnt Orange
Alnus serrulata (Common or Smooth Alder)[1]	Roots	Brown
	Bark	Yellow to golden brown
	Leaves	Yellow-green
Baptisia tinctoria (False Indigo—Rattleweed) (has yellow flowers)	Leaves & stems	Blue
Galium tinctorium var. *floridanum* (Bedstraw)	Roots	Yellow, Red, Red-orange
Helianthus angustifolius	Flowers	Yellow
Helianthus atrorubens (Sunflowers)	Flowers	
Juniperus virginiana (Red Cedar)	Inner bark	Mahogany
Plantago virginica	Leaves & roots	Green
Plantago virginica var. *viridescens*	Leaves & roots	Green
Prunus americana (American Wild Plum)	Inner bark and fruits	Reddish brown
Prunus angustifolia (Chickasaw Plum)	Inner bark and fruits	Reddish brown
Prunus serotina (Black Cherry)	Inner bark	Yellow-orange, red-orange, tan
	Roots	Blue-violet
Quercus (Red and Black Oaks)		
Quercus velutina (Black Oak)	Inner bark	Yellow-brown
Quercus nigra (Water Oak)	Inner bark	Light brown—brown
Quercus laurifolia (Laurel Oak)	Inner bark	Light brown—brown
Quercus Phellos (Willow Oak)	Inner bark	Light brown—brown
Quercus laevis (Turkey Oak)	Inner bark	Light brown—brown

Oak bark used by Indians both as a dye and a mordant for setting the colors of other colors. If used alone oak bark sets its own color.

---

[1] No mordant required. Dyes both vegetable and animal fibers.

PLANT	PARTS USED	COLORS OF DYES
Rhus copallina (Dwarf or Shining Sumac)	Ripe berries	Beige, dark tan
Rumex verticillatus (Sorrel-Swamp or Water Dock)	Stalks and leaves	Gray-blue
Sanguinaria canadensis var. *rotundifolia* (Bloodroot—"Red Puccoon")	Roots	Yellow-orange

One of the best known Indian dye plants. Doesn't need a mordant and can be used on both animal and vegetable fibers. Used by Indians to paint faces or as a rouge.

Sassafras albidum var. *molle* (Red Sassafras)	Bark of root	Rose-brown
Solidago hispida var. *pulverulenta*	Flowers	Yellow-orange
Solidago stricta	Flowers	Yellow-orange
Solidago salicina	Flowers	Yellow-orange
Solidago odora	Flowers	Yellow-orange
Solidago tortifolia	Flowers	Yellow-orange
Solidago fistulosa	Flowers	Yellow-orange
Symplocos tinctoria (Florida Laurel, Horse-Sugar) (has fragrant flowers)	Leaves and inner bark	Yellow
Vaccinium elliottii and *Vaccinium tenellum* (Blueberries)	Fruit	Gray, blue, purple

Color self setting—needs no mordant.

Vitis rotundifolia	Fruit	Blue
Vitis cinerea var. *floridana*	Fruit	Blue
Vitis vulpina (Wild Grapes)	Fruit	Blue

FLOWERING AND OTHER DECORATIVE OR DISTINCTIVE INDIGENOUS TREES, SHRUBS, VINES AND OTHER PLANTS WHICH IN THEIR NATURAL ASSOCIATIONS COULD HAVE BEEN OBSERVED BY THE FRENCH AND THE EASTERN TIMUCUANS IN 1562–68

Undoubtedly the French under Ribault when first reaching the shores of Florida and the St. Johns River area must have been astounded at the number and variety of flowering and fragrant plants, vines, shrubs, and trees which confronted them. The time of year was such that they met with much the same dazzling glory of the flora that greeted Ponce de León when he first set foot on the land he named Florida, slightly north of the point where St. Augustine is now situated. Luxuriant masses of blue, crimson, pink, and yellow flowers, the coral berries, azaleas, palmettos, flowering magnolias, and other colorful and scented flora must have made a very pleasing and startling background for the French landings.

Outstanding among the flora of that time undoubtedly were many of the following which, with their associates, warrant a place (site conditions permitting or upon preparation of suitable site conditions), from a decorative or other distinctive point of view in the area set aside for memorializing Fort Caroline:

A. TREES

Aesculus pavia (Red Buckeye)
Amelanchier intermedia (Swamp Serviceberry)
Angelica vennosa (Angelica-Tree)
Aralia spinosa (Devil's Walking-Stick)
Asimina triloba (North American Paw-Paw)
Callicarpa americana (French Mulberry)
Carpinus caroliniana (Hornbeam)
Carya aquatica (Swamp Hickory)
Carya glabra (Pignut Hickory)
Carya tomentosa (Mockernut Hickory)
Castanea pumila (Chinquapin)
Catalpa bignoides (Catalpa)
Celtis occidentalis (Hackberry)
Celtis laevigata (Hackberry)
Cercis canadensis (Redbud)
Chamaecyparis thyoides (White Cedar)
Chionanthus virginicus (Fringe Tree)
Cornus florida (Flowering Dogwood)
Crataegus flava (Summer Haw)
Crataegus marshallii (Parsley-leaved Thorn)
Crataegus viridis (Southern Thorn)
Diospyros virginiana (Persimmon)
Gleditsia aquatica (Water Locust)
Gleditsia triacanthos (Honey Locust)
Gordonia lasianthus (Loblolly Bay)
Halesia carolina (Silver Bell Tree)
Hamamelis virginica (Witch Hazel)
Hex opaca (American Holly)
Juniperus silicicola (Southern Red Cedar)
Laurocerasus caroliniana (Wild Orange, Cherry Laurel)
Liriodendron tulipifera (Tulip Tree)
Magnolia grandiflora (Bull Bay, Southern Magnolia)
Magnolia macrophylla (Large-leaved Umbrella Tree)
Magnolia pyramidata (Rhombil-leaved Umbrella Tree)
Magnolia virginiana (Sweet Bay)
Malus angustifolia (Southern Crabapple)
Myrica cerifera (Wax-Myrtle)
Nyssa aquatica (Water Tupelo)
Nyssa oqeche (Ogeche Lime or Plum)
Nyssa sylvatica (Sour Gum, Tupelo)
Osmanthus americanus (Devil Wood)
Oxydendron arboreum (Sour Wood, Lily of the Valley Tree)
Persea borbonia (Red Bay)

A. TREES (Continued)
  Persea pubescens (Swamp Red Bay)
  Pinckneya pubens (Fever Tree)
  Pinus taeda (Loblolly Pine)
  Planera aquatica (Water Elm)
  Plantanus occidentalis (Sycamore)
  Prunus americana (Wild Yellow Plum)
  Prunus angustifolia (Chickasaw Plum)
  Prunus serotina (Black Cherry)
  Prunus umbellata (Black Sloe)
  Ptelea monophylla (Buckwheat Tree, Titi)
  Quercus phellos (Willow Oak)
  Quercus virginiana (Live Oak)
  Sabal palmetto (Cabbage Palmetto)
  Sassafras albidum (Sassafras)
  Serenoa serrulata (Saw Palmetto)
  Taxodium ascendens (Pond Cypress)
  Taxodium distichum (Bald Cypress)
  Vibirnum rufidulum (Southern Black Haw)
  Zanthoxylum clava-herculis (Pepperwood)
B. SHRUBS
  Ascyrum hypericoides (St. Peter's-wort)
  Ascyrum tetrapethlum (St. Peter's-wort)
  Baccharis halimifolia (Sea Myrtle)
  Befaria racemosa (Tar-Flower)
  Bumelia reclinata (Buckthorn)
  Bumelia tenax (Buckthorn)
  Callicarpa americana (French Mulberry)
  Calycanthus floridus (Flowering Caroline Allspice)
  Ceanothus americanus (New Jersey Tea)
  Cephalanthus occidentalis (Buttonbush)
  Ceratiola ericoides (Florida Rosemary)
  Chionanthus virginicus (Fringe tree, Graybeard)
  Cornus asperifolia (Rough-leaved Cornel)
  Cornus stricta (Stiff Cornel)
  Crookea microsepala (Crookea)
  Cyrilla racemiflora (Titi)
  Forestiera porpulosa (Florida Privet)
  Hibiscus moscheutos (Rose Mallow)
  Hydrangea arborescens var. *oblonga* (Wild Hydrangea)
  Hypericum aspalathoides (St. John's-wort)
  Hypericum fasciculatum (St. John's-wort)
  Hypericum myrtiflorum (St. John's-wort)
  Illicium floridanum (Star Anise)
  Illicium parviflorum (Star Anise)
  Ilex cassine (Dahoon Holly)
  Ilex coriacea (Sweet Gallberry) (said to be edible)
  Ilex glabra (Inkberry)
  Ilex myrtifolia (Myrtle-leaved Holly)
  Ilex vomitoria (Yaupon)
  Jussiaea leptocarpa (Primrose Willow)
  Jussiaea peruviana (Primrose Willow)
  Jussiaea scabra (Primrose Willow)
  Kalmia hirsuta (Dwarf Kalmia)

B. SHRUBS (Continued)
>   *Lespedeza violacea* (Violet Bush Clover)
>   *Leucothoë racemosa* (Fetterbush)
>   *Liquidambar styraciflua* (Sweet Gum)
>   *Lindera benzoin* (Wild Allspice)
>   *Lonicera sempervirens* (Coral Honeysuckle)
>   *Lyonia lucida* (Tetterbush)
>   *Lyonia mariana* (Staggerbush)
>   *Myrica heterophylla* (Wax Myrtle)
>   *Myrica pusilla* (Dwarf Wax Myrtle)
>   *Nyssa sylvatica* (Black Gum)
>   *Osmanthus americanus* (Wild Olive)
>   *Persea littoralis* (Bay-bush)
>   *Rhododendron serrulatum* (Saw-toothed Azalea)
>   *Rhododendron viscosum* (Azalea)
>   *Rhus copallina* (Dwarf Sumac)
>   *Styrax pulverulenta* (Storax)
>   *Vaccinium arboreum* (Sparkleberry)
>   *Vaccinium nitidum* (Blueberry)
>   *Vaccinium stamineum* (Deerberry)
>   *Viburnum cassinoides* (Withe Rod)
>   *Viburnum obovatum* (Small viburnum)
>   *Viburnum semitomentosum* (Viburnum)
>   *Wisteria frutescens* (American Wisteria)
>   *Xolisma ferruginea* (Crooked-Wood)
>   *Xolisma foliosiflora* (Crooked-Wood)
>   *Xolisma fruticosa* (Crooked-Wood)
>   *Yucca aloifolia* (Spanish Dagger)
>   *Yucca gloriosa* (Spanish Bayonet)
>   *Yucca smalliana* (Adam's Needle)

C. VINES
>   *Ampelopsis arborea* (Pepper-vine)
>   *Berchemia scandens* (Rattan-vine)
>   *Bignonia capreolata* (Cross-vine)
>   *Campsis radicans* (Trumpet Flower)
>   *Decumaria barbara* (Climbing Hydrangea)
>   *Epigaea repens* (Trailing Arbutus, Mayflower, Ground Laurel)
>   *Gelsemium sempervirens* (Yellow Jessamine, Evening Trumpet-Flower)
>   *Ipomea littoralis* (Morning Glory)
>   *Ipomea pandurata* (Wild-Potato-Vine)
>   *Lonicera sempervirens* (Trumpet—Coral Honeysuckle)
>   *Melothria pendula* (Creeping cucumber)
>   *Parthenocissus quinquefolia* (Virginia Creeper)
>   *Passiflora incarnata* (Apricot Vine)
>   *Rosa setigera* (Prairie Rose)
>   *Smilax walteri* (Red-berried Bamboo)
>   *Valeriana scandens* (Climbing Valerian)
>   *Viorna crispa* (Blue Jasmine)
>   *Viorna reticulata* (Leather Flower)

D. OTHER PLANTS
>   *Actinospermum angustifolium* (Marigold)
>   *Agave virginica* (American Aloe)
>   *Amorpha fruticosa* (False Indigo)
>   *Amphicarpa bracteata* (Hog Peanut)

Appendix D—Wilder   201

D. OTHER PLANTS (Continued)

Amsonia ciliata (Amsonia)
Amsonia rigida (Amsonia)
Angelica venenosa (Hairy Angelica)
Apios americana (Groundnut)
Apocynum cannabinum (Indian Hemp)
Argemone alba (Prickly Poppy)
Argemone mexicana (Prickly Poppy)
Arisaema dracontium (Dragon Root, Green Dragon)
Aristolochia serpentaria (Virginia Snake Root)
Asclepias variegata (White Milkweed)
Asclepias viridiflora (Green Milkweed)
Asimina parviflora (Custard Apple, Paw paw)
Asimina angustifolia (Custard Apple, Paw paw)
Asimina pygmaea (Custard Apple, Paw paw)
Aster adnatus (Aster)
Aster carolinianus (Aster)
Aster concolor (Aster)
Aster elliottii (Aster)
Aster grandiflorus (Large-Flowered Aster)
Aster patens (Late purple Aster)
Aster puniceus (Purple Stemmed Aster)
Aster walteri (Aster)
Atamosco atamasco (Atomasco Lily)
Atamosco treatiae (Rain Lily)
Baptisia lanceolata (False Indigo)
Baptisia tinctoria (Wild Indigo)
Berlandiera subacaulis (Florida dandelion)
Berlandiera pumila (Florida dandelion)
Bidens leucantha (Spanish needles)
Bidens mitis (Bur-marigold)
Blephariglottis ciliaris (Fringed Orchid)
Blephariglottis conspicua (Fringed Orchid)
Borrichia frutescens (Sea Ox-eye)
Bradburya virginiana (Spurred Butterfly Pea)
Brasenia schreberi (Watershield or Purple Bonnet)
Cabomba caroliniana (Watershield or Fanwort)
Callirrhoë papaver (Poppy Mallow)
Campanula americana (Tall Bell Flower)
Campanula floridana (Bell Flower)
Canavalia obtusifolia (Beach Bean)
Canna flaccida (Golden Canna, Indian Shot)
Cardamine bulbosa (Spring Cress)
Cassia fasciculata (Patridge Pea)
Cassia ligustrina (Wild Senna)
Castalia odorata (Pond Lily)
Castilleja coccinea (Painted Cup)
Chamaecrista brachiata (Partridge Pea)
Chaptalia tomentosa (Pineland Daisy)
Chelone obliqua (Southern Turtlehead)
Chrysogonum virginianum (Chrysogonum)
Chrysopsis graminifolia (Golden Aster)
Chrysopsis mariana (Maryland Golden Aster)
Chrysopsis nervosa (Golden Aster)

D. OTHER PLANTS (Continued)

Cicuta curtissii (Water Hemlock)
Clinopodium coccineum (Basil)
Clitoria mariana (Butterfly Pea)
Collinsonia canadensis (Horse Balm)
Convolvulus sepium (Hedge Bindweed)
Convolvulus sepium repens (Narrow-leaved Bindweed)
Corallorhiza wisteriana (Coral-Root)
Coreopsis auriculata (Coreopsis)
Coreopsis lanceolata (Lance-leaved Tickseed)
Coreopsis leavenworthii (Coreopsis)
Coreopsis longifolia (Coreopsis)
Coreopsis major stellata (Common Tickseed)
Coreopsis pubescens (Coreopsis)
Crinum americanum (Crinum or Florida Swamp Lily, St. John's Lily)
Crotalaria maritima (Rattlebox)
Crotalaria sagittalis (Rattlebox)
Cynoglossum virginianum (Wild Comfrey)
Dasystoma pectinata (False Foxglove)
Decodon verticillatus (Swamp Loosestrife)
Dendropogon usneoides (Spanish Moss)
Dicerandra linearifolia (Dicerandra)
Doellingeria reticulata (White Top Aster)
Drosera rotundifolia (Round-leaved Sundew)
Epidendrum conopseum (Greenfly orchid)
Erigeron philadelphicus (Daisy Fleabane)
Erigeron quercifolius (Fleabane)
Erigeron vernus (Fleabane)
Eriogonum floridanum (Wild Buckwheat)
Eriogonum tomentosum (Wild Buckwheat)
Erythrina herbacea (Cherokee Bean)
Erythronium americanum (Yellow Dogstooth-violet)
Eupatorium hyssopifolium (Thoroughwort)
Eupatorium perfoliatum (Boneset)
Eupatorium pilosum (Rough Thoroughwort)
Euphorbia corollata (Flowering Spurge)
Euphorbia heterophylla (Painted Leaf)
Euphorbia pinetorum (Wild Poinsetta)
Gaillardia lanceolata (Gaillardia)
Gerardia fasciculata (Gerardia)
Gerardia filifolia (Gerardia)
Gerardia maritima (Gerardia)
Gerardia parvifolia (Gerardia)
Gerardia purpurea (Gerardia)
Gilia rubra (Red Gilia)
Gnaphalium obtusifolium (Everlasting)
Gnaphalium obtusifolium Helleri (Everlasting)
Goodyera pubescens (Downy Rattlesnake Platain)
Gratiola aurea (Hedge Hyssop)
Gymnadeniopsis nivea (White Spurred Orchid)
Habenaria ciliaris (Yellow Fringed Orchid)
Habenaria distans (Spider Orchid)
Habenaria nivea (Snowy Orchid)
Habenaria quinqueseta (Spider Orchid)

D. OTHER PLANTS (Continued)

Habenaria repens (Spider Orchid)
Helenium autumnale parviflorum (Sneezeweed)
Helenium tenuifolium (Spanish Daisy)
Helenium vernale (Sneezeweed)
Helianthemum arenicola (Rock Rose)
Helianthemum carolinianum (Rock Rose)
Helianthemum corymbosum (Rock Rose)
Helianthemum nashii (Rock Rose)
Helianthus agrestis (Sunflower)
Helianthus angustifolius (Swamp Sunflower)
Helianthus debilis (Beach Sunflower)
Helianthus simulans (Sunflower)
Heliotropium curassavicum (Seaside Heliotrope)
Hepatica americana (Round-leaved Hepatica)
Hexalectris spicata (Crested Carolroot)
Hibiscus aculeatus (Hibiscus, Rose Mallow)
Hibiscus coccineus (Hibiscus, Rose Mallow)
Hibiscus furcellatus (Hibiscus, Rose Mallow)
Hibiscus grandiflorus (Hibiscus, Rose Mallow)
Hibiscus incanus (Hibiscus, Rose Mallow)
Hibiscus moscheutos (Swamp Rose Mallow)
Hieracium gronovii (Hawkweed)
Hieracium venosum (Rattlesnake Weed)
Houstonia angustifolia (Diamond Flower)
Houstonia rotundifolia (Diamond Flower)
Hymenocallis rotatum (Spider Lily)
Hypoxis hirsuta (Yellow star-grass)
Hypoxis juncea (Yellow star-grass)
Ibidium beckii (Ladies' Tresses)
Ibidium cernuum (Ladies' Tresses)
Ibidium praecox (Ladies' Tresses)
Impatiens capensis or otherwise called *biflora* (Spotted Touch-me-not)
Indigofera caroliniana (Wild Indigo)
Iris hexagona (Southern Blue Flag)
Jussiaea repens (Primrose-willow)
Kosteletzkya virginica (Small Rose Mallow)
Krameria secundiflora (Krameria)
Lespedeza frutescens (Bush Clover)
Lespedeza hirta appressipilis (Bush Clover)
Leucothoë acuminata (Leucothoe)
Leucothoë racemosa (Leucothoe)
Liatris elegans (Southern Blazing Star)
Lilium catesbaei (Leopard or Pine Lily)
Lilium michauxii (Carolina Lily)
Limodorum multiflorum (Terrestrial orchid)
Limodorum parviflorum (Terrestrial orchid)
Limodorum simpsonii (Terrestrial orchid)
Limodorum tuberosum (Terrestrial orchid)
Limonium carolinianum (Marsh Rosemary or Sea Lavender)
Linaria canadensis (Blue Toad-Flax)
Linaria floridana (Blue Toad-Flax)
Listera australis (Southern Twayblade)
Lobelia cardinalis (Cardinal Flower)

D. OTHER PLANTS (Continued)
    Lobelia feayana (Lobelia)
    Lobelia glandulosa (Lobelia)
    Lobelia paludosa (Lobelia)
    Lobelia puberula (Lobelia)
    Lobelia xalapensis (Lobelia)
    Ludwigia alternifolia (Seedbox)
    Ludwigia brevipes (Short-stalked Seedbox)
    Ludwigia natans (Floating Flase Loosestrife)
    Ludwigia virgata (Wandlike False Loosestrife)
    Lupinus diffusus (Lupine)
    Lupinus nuttallii (Lupine)
    Lupinus perennis (Wild Lupine)
    Lupinus villosus (Lupine)
    Lygodesmia aphylla (Roserush)
    Lythrum lanceolatum (Loosestrife)
    Medeola virginiana (Indian Cucumber-root)
    Melanthium virginicum (Bunch Flower)
    Micromeria pilosiuscula (Micromeria)
    Mikania scandens (Climbing Hempweed)
    Mimulus alatus (Monkey Flower)
    Mitchella repens (Partridge Berry)
    Monarda punctata (Horse-Mint)
    Nelumbo lutea (Water chinquapin or American Lotus Lily)
    Nymphaea macrophylla (Cow Lily)
    Nymphaea odorata (White Water Lily)
    Nymphoides aquatica (Floating-Heart)
    Oenothera biennis (Evening Primrose)
    Oenothera fruticosa (Sundrops)
    Oenothera humifusa (Evening Primrose)
    Oenothera laciniata (Evening Primrose)
    Onosmodium virginianum (False Gromwell)
    Orontium acquaticum (Golden Club)
    Oxalis violacea (Violet Wood Sorrel)
    Pogonia ophioglossoides (Rose Pogonia)
    Pogonia divaricata (Rose Pogonia)
    Pavonia spinifex (Yellow Pavonia)
    Pedicularis canadensis (Wood Betony)
    Peltandra sagittaefolia (Spoonflower)
    Penstemon australis (Beard tongue)
    Penstemon multiflorus (Beard tongue)
    Phlox divaricata Laphamii (Wild Blue Phlox)
    Phlox nivales (Phlox)
    Phlox pilosa (Hairy Phlox)
    Pinguicula elatior (Butterwort)
    Pinguicula lutea (Butterwort)
    Pinguicula pumila (Butterwort)
    Physalis maritima (Maritime Ground Cherry)
    Physalis pruinosa (Strawberry-Tomato)
    Physalis pubescens (Ground Cherry)
    Polygala cruciata (Marsh Milkwort)
    Polygala lutea (Orange Milkwort)
    Polygala polygama (Racemed Milkwort)
    Polygala ramosa (Pine-barren Milkwort)

D. OTHER PLANTS (Continued)

Polygala rugelii (Thimbles, Bachelor's-buttons)
Polygonatum biflorum (Hairy Solomons-seal)
Polygonum sagittatum (Arrow-leaved Tearthumb)
Pontederia (Pickerelweed)
    P. cordata
    P. lanceolata
Prenanthes virgata (Nabalus)
Ratibida pinnata (Grayheaded Cone-Flower)
Rhexia (Deergrass, Meadow-beauty)
    R. ciliosa
    R. lutea
    R. mariana
    R. mariana purpurea
    R. virginicia septemnervia
Rivina humilis (Bloodberry)
Rosa carolina (Carolina Rose)
Rosa palustris (Swamp Rose)
Rudbeckia divergens (Cone-Flower)
Rudbeckia glabra (Cone-Flower)
Rudbeckia laciniata (Tall Cone-Flower)
Ruellia caroliniensis semiclava (Ruellia)
Ruellia ciliosa (Ruellia)
Ruellia humilis (Ruellia)
Ruellia parviflora (Ruellia)
Ruellia pinctorum (Ruellia)
Sabatia angularis (Rose-Pink)
Sabatia calycina (Marsh Pink)
Sabatia decandra (Marsh Pink)
Sabatia dodecandra (Large Marsh Pink)
Sabatia elliotti (Marsh Pink)
Sabatia grandiflora (Marsh Pink)
Sabatia lanceolata (Marsh Pink)
Sabatia stellaris (Sea-Pink)
Sagittaria falcata (Arrowhead)
Sagittaria latifolia pubescens (Arrowhead)
Sagittaria lyrata (Arrowhead)
Salpingostylis coelestina (Bartram's Ixia)
Salvia azurea (Sage)
Salvia coccinea (Sage)
Salvia lyrata (Sage)
Samolus ebracteatus (Primrose)
Samolus floribundus (Primrose)
Sanguinaria canadensis rotundifolia (Bloodroot)
Sarracenia drummondii (Pitcher Plant, Trumpet Leaf)
Sarracenia flava (Trumpets)
Sarracenia minor (Pitcher Plant, Trumpet Leaf)
Sarracenia psittacina (Pitcher Plant, Trumpet Leaf)
Saururus cernuus (Swamp Lily, Lizard's Tail)
Sclerolepis uniflora (Sclerolepis)
Scoparia dulcis (Sweet Broom)
Scutellaria arenicola (Skullcap)
Scutellaria integrifolia (Skullcap)
Scutellaria multiglandulosa (Skullcap)

D. OTHER PLANTS (Continued)
  Senecio aureus (Golden Ragwort)
  Senecio glabellus (Ragwort)
  Sericocarpus asteroides (White-topped Aster)
  Sericocarpus bifoliatus (White-topped Aster)
  Sisyrinchium angustifolium (Blue-eyed Grass)
  Sitilias caroliniana (False Dandelion)
  Solanum aculeatissimum (Horse-Nettle)
  Solidago caesia (Wreath Goldenrod)
  Solidago chapmanii (Goldenrod)
  Solidago fistulosa (Goldenrod)
  Solidago puberula (Downy Goldenrod)
  Solidago sempervirens (Goldenrod)
  Specularia perfoliata (Venus's Looking-Glass)
  Spigelia marilandica (Indian Pink)
  Spiranthes cernua (Ladies' Tresses)
  Strophostyles helvola (Wild Bean)
  Tephrosia virginiana (Goat's Rue)
  Teucrium nashii (Germander)
  Teucrium occidentale (Wood Sage)
  Thalia dealbata (Arrowroot)
  Thalia geniculata (Arrowroot)
  Trichostema dichotomum (Blue Curls)
  Trichostema suffrutescens (Blue Curls)
  Uvularia perfoliata (Bellwort)
  Verbena bonariensis (Verbena)
  Verbena caroliniensis (Verbena)
  Verbena hastata (Blue Vervain)
  Verbena tampensis (Verbena)
  Verbena tenuisecta (Verbena)
  Verbesina laciniata (Crown Beard)
  Veronicastrum virginicum (Culver's Root)
  Vigna repens (Wild Pea)
  Viola floridana (Violet)
  Viola lanceolata (Lance-leaved Violet)
  Viola palmata (Early Blue Violet)
  Viola primulifolia (Violet)
  Viola septemloba (Violet)
  Viola vittata (Violet)
  Viorna baldwinii (Dwarf Clematis)
  Xyris flexuosa (Yellow-eyed Grass)
   X. ambigua
   X. curtissii
   X. fimbriata
   X. difformis
   X. platylepis
   X. Smalliana

Baker, Mary Francis. *Florida Wild Flowers.* New York, 1938.

Dan, Frederick W. *Florida Old and New.* New York, 1934.

Dovell, J. E. *Florida: Historic, Dramatic, Contemporary.* Vol. 1. New York, 1952.

Fernald, M. L. *Gray's Manual of Botany.* New York, 1950.

Florida Forest and Park Service. *Common Forest Trees of Florida.* Tallahassee, 1943.

Hakluyt, Richard. *Hakluyt's Collection of the Early Voyages, Travels, and Discoveries of the English Nation.* Vol. 3. London, 1810.

Hanna, Kathryn Abbey. *Florida: Land of Change.* Chapel Hill, N.C., 1948.

Harlow and Harrar. *Textbook of Dendrology.* New York, 1958.

Harper, Francis. *The Travels of William Bartram.* Naturalists' Edition. New Haven, Conn., 1958.

Harper, Roland M. "Geography and Vegetation of Florida." Sixth Annual Report of the Florida State Geological Survey. Tallahassee, 1914.

Hedrick, U. P. *A History of Horticulture in America to 1860.* New York, 1950.

Kenny, Michael. *The Romance of the Floridas.* New York, 1934.

Kurtz, Herman. "Florida Dunes and Scrub-Vegetation and Geology." Florida State Geological Survey Bulletin no. 23. Tallahassee, 1942.

———. *Tidal Marshes of the Gulf and Atlantic Coasts of Northern Florida and Charleston, S.C.* Tallahassee, 1957.

Leechman, John Douglas. *Vegetable Dyes from North American Plants.* St. Paul, Minn., 1945.

Le Moyne, Jacques. *Narrative of Le Moyne.* Translated by Fred B. Perkins. Boston, 1875.

Le Moyne, Jacques. *Voyages en Virginie et en Floride.* Paris, 1927.

Monardes, Nicholas (Physician of Seville, 1574). *Joeful Newses out of the Newe Founde Worlde.* Tudor Translations. New York, 1925.

Nehring, Henry. *The Plant World in Florida.* New York, 1933.

Rollins, Reed C. *Edible Wild Plants of Eastern North America.* New York, 1958.

Safford, W. E. "Narcotic Plants and Stimulants of the Ancient Americans." Annual Report of the Smithsonian Institution for 1916, pp. 387–424. Washington, 1917.

Shipp, Bernard. *The History of Hernando de Sota and Florida, or Record of the Events of Fifty-six Years from 1512 to 1568.* Philadelphia, 1881.

Solís de Merás, Gonzalo. *Pedro Menéndez de Avilés.* Translated by Jeannette Thurber Connor. DeLand, Fla., 1923.

Stone, Eric. *Medicine among American Indians.* New York, 1932.

Taylor, Lyda Averill. *Plants Used as Curatives by Certain Southeastern Tribes.* Cambridge, Mass., 1940.

Van Dersal, William R. *Native Woody Plants of the United States.* Washington, 1938.

Wyly, Francis D. *Palms and Flowers of Florida.* Pass-a-Grille, Fla., 1940.

Notes

Notes to Introduction

1. Spelled as "Ribauld" in the explorer's own *The Whole and True Discouerye of Terra Florida* (London: Rowland Hall for Thomas Hacket, 1563), and as "Ribaut" in Jean Ribaut, *The Whole and True Discouerye of Terra Florida,* a Facsimile Reprint of the London Edition of 1563, together with a Transcript of an English Version in the British Museum with Notes by H. P. Biggar and a Biography [of Ribaut] by Jeannette Thurber Connor (Deland: Florida State Historical Society, 1927; reprinted in facsimile with an introduction by David L. Dowd, Gainesville: University of Florida Press, 1964), 3. However, several sixteenth-century manuscripts bearing the explorer's signature show that the correct spelling is "Ribault." Photocopies of these manuscripts can be seen at Fort Caroline National Memorial, Jacksonville, Fla. See also note 1 to Dowd's introduction to the 1964 edition of *Whole and True Discouerye,* 1927, *lii*.

2. E. R. G. Taylor, *The Mathematical Practitioners of Tudor and Stuart England* (Cambridge: At the University Press, 1954), 16; and E. R. G. Taylor, *The Haven Finding Art* (New York: Abelard-Schuman, 1957), 194.

3. Connor's biography in *Whole and True Discouerye,* 1927, 4.

4. Francis Parkman, *Pioneers of France in the New World* (Boston: Little, Brown & Co., 1891), 35–39.

5. Ibid, 39–47.

6. Henry Folmer, *Franco-Spanish Rivalry in North America, 1524–1763* (Glendale, Calif.: Arthur H. Clark Co., 1953), 32–40.

7. Ibid., 53, 58–61.

8. Ibid., 73–75.

9. Ibid., 21–22, 25, 33, 35.

10. Ibid., 44–45, 53, 68–70.

11. Woodbury Lowery, *The Spanish Settlements within the Present Limits of the United States, 1513–1561* (New York: Russell & Russell, 1959), 134–43, 157–60, 164–68, 176–88, 218–26, 358–75, 417–26.

12. Connor's biography in Ribaut, *Whole and True Discouerye,* 1927, 8, 9–11.

13. Printed in London by Rowland Hall for Thomas Hacket.

14. As "The True and Last Discoverie of Florida" in Richard Hakluyt, *Divers Voyages Touching the Discovery of America and the Islands Adjacent,* edited by J. W. Jones (London, 1850).

15. DeLand: Florida State Historical Society.

16. Gainesville: University of Florida Press, 1964.

17. Charles E. Bennett, *Laudonnière and Fort Caroline* (Gainesville: University of Florida Press, 1964), 7, 9.

18. John Sparke, Jr., "The Voyage Made by M. John Hawkins, Esq.," in Richard Hakluyt, *Collection of the Early Voyages, Travels, and Discoveries of the English Nation,* edited by R. H. Evans (London, 1810–12), 3:615.

19. *Coppie d'une lettre venant de La Floride. envoyée à Rouen* (Paris: Vincent Norment & Jeanne Bruneau, 1565).

20. Bennett, *Laudonnière,* 65–70.

21. Parkman, *Pioneers,* 93–94, 97–103, 113.

22. Ibid., 114–24, 131–47.

23. Ibid., 124–26, 128–30.

24. *Discours de l'histoire de la Floride, contenant le trahison des Espagnols, contre les sujets du Roy* (Dieppe: Sellier, 1566); *Discours de l'histoire de la Floride, contenant la cruauté des Espagnols, contre les sujets du Roy* (Dieppe, 1566); *Discours et histoire de ce qui est advenu en la Floride* (France, 1566); and *Histoire mémorable du dernier voyage aux Indes, lieu appelé la Floride* (Lyons: Jean Saugrain, 1566).

25. *A True and Perfect Description, of the Last Voyage or Navigation Attempted by . . . Frenchmen, into Terra Florida* (London: Henry Denham for Thomas Hacket, 1566).

26. "Bref discours et histoire d'un voyage de quelques Fran-

çois en la Floride," in the Urban Chauveton edition of Girolamo Benzoni, *Histoire nouvelle du Nouveau Monde* (Geneva: Eustace Vignon, 1579).

27. "De Gallorum Expeditione in Floridam," in the Chauveton edition of Benzoni, *Novae Novi Orbis Historiae* (Geneva: Eustathium Vignon, 1578).

28. "Historien von der Frantzösen Zug unnd Reyss in die Landtschaft Floridam genannt," in *Der newenn Weldt und Indianischen Niedergaengischen Koenigreichs, Newe und Wahrhaffte History* (Basel: S. Henricpetri, 1583); and "Kurtze Historia von der Frantzösen Ruestung und Zug in die Provintz oder Land Floridam," in Benzoni, *Novae Novi Orbis Historiae, Das is, Aller Geschichten, So in der newen Welt welche Occidentalia India . . . genent wird* (Helmstedt: Jacobum Luicium, 1590).

29. *The New World* (New York: Duell, Sloan & Pearce, 1946).

30. *Brevis Narratio Eorum Quae in Florida Americae Provincia* (Frankfurt-am-Main, De Bry). A first edition of this Latin version is at Fort Caroline National Memorial.

31. Theodore de Bry, ed., *Der ander Theyl, der Newlich erfundenen Landtschafft von dreyen Schiffahrten so die Frantzösen in Floridam* (Frankfurt-am-Main: D. von Bry, 1591).

32. As *Narrative of Le Moyne* (Boston: James R. Osgood & Co.). This work also is available at Fort Caroline National Memorial.

33. Charles E. Bennett, comp., *Settlement of Florida* (Gainesville: University of Florida Press, 1968).

34. Lorant, *The New World.*

35. By Martine Basanier (Paris: Guillaume Auvray). The museum of Fort Caroline National Memorial has this first edition and also a modern facsimile of it.

36. Paris: Guiraudet & Jouaust for the P. Jannet Library.

37. As *A Notable History Containing Foure Voyages Made by* Certaine French Captaines unto Florida (London: Thomas Dawson).

38. "A Notable Historie . . ." in Richard Hakluyt, *The Principal Navigations, Voyages, Traffiques, and Discoveries of the English Nation* (London: George Bishop, Ralph Newberie & Robert Barker, 1598–1600) 3:301–60; Hakluyt, *op. cit.* (Glasgow: J. MacLehose, 1904), vol. 9, and *A Notable History . . .* (Larchmont, N.Y.: Henry Stevens, Son, & Stiles, 1964),

which is a facsimile of the 1587 book with an introductory essay by Thomas R. Adams, outlining the principal sources of the sixteenth-century French voyages to Florida.

39. In *Ensayo cronológico para la historia general de la Florida* (Madrid: Nicolás Rodríguez Franco, 1723).

40. By Eugenio Ruidíaz y Caravia, ed., *La Florida: su conquista y colonización por Pedro Menéndez de Avilés*, 2 vols. (Madrid: J. A. García, 1893), 1:1–320.

41. As *Pedro Menéndez de Avilés: Adelantado, Governor and Captain General of Florida* (DeLand: Florida State Historical Society, 1923).

42. Gainesville: University of Florida Press, 1964.

43. By Henri Ternaux-Compans, *Voyages, relations et mémoires originaux pour servir à l'histoire de la découverte de l'Amérique*, 20 vols. (Paris: A. Bertrand, 1837–41), vol. 20: *Recueil de pièces sur la Floride*, 165–232. The Spanish title of the narrative is "Memoria del buen suceso y buen viaje que Dios, nuestro Señor, fué servido de dar a la armada que salió de la ciudad de Cádiz para la provincia y costa de la Florida, de la cual fué por general el ilustre señor Pero Menéndez de Avilés, comendador de la Orden de Santiago."

44. D. J. F. Pacheco, D. F. de Cárdenas, and D. L. Torres de Mendoza, eds., *Colección de documentos ineditos relativos al descubrimiento, conquista y colonización de las antiguas posesiones españolas de América y Oceanía* (Madrid), 3:441–79.

45. *La Florida*, 2:431–65.

46. *Historical Collections of Louisiana and Florida*, 2d series (New York), 191–234.

47. *Old South Leaflets*, no. 89 (Boston, 1896).

48. Bennett, *Laudonnière*, 141–63.

49. In Genaro García, ed., *Dos antiguas relaciones de la Florida* (México: J. Aguilar Vera y Compañía, 1902), 1–152.

50. As *Pedro Menéndez de Avilés, Founder of Florida* (Gainesville: University of Florida Press, 1965).

51. Bennett, *Laudonnière*, 49.

52. Ibid., 50–52.

53. Département de Seine-et-Oise, Ville de Saint-Germain-en-Laye, Registre des Actes de Décès, no. 1185 (1574). We are indebted to Mlle Salomé Mandel of Paris, who found this record. Translated into English, the French text reads: "On Saturday, the twenty-fourth, Captain de Laudonnière died and

was buried on Sunday, and his services were performed on the Monday following."

Notes to Three Voyages

1. From man's beginnings to the birth of Christ it took millions of years for the human population of the earth to reach 300 million people. From the birth of Christ to the time of Laudonnière it took only 1,500 years to reach 500 million people. From the time of Laudonnière until today it has taken but 400 years to reach the present figure of 3 billion people on earth. By 1982 the population figure is expected to reach 5 billion people. See Don Fabun, *The Dynamics of Change* (Englewood Cliffs, N.J.: Prentice-Hall, 1967), 12.

2. Called today the Azores.

3. Called today the Canary Islands.

4. Off Newfoundland.

5. The French word used was *laurier*, which included laurel and magnolia (or bay). Hakluyt variously translated it as "laurel" and "bay." *Magnolia grandiflora*, commonly called magnolia, and *Magnolia virginiana*, commonly called bay, are both prevalent in the area. A settler would probably be much more impressed with the spectacular beauty and fragrance of the *M. grandiflora* than with any of its relatives carrying the same family name.

6. The fruit tree to which he referred was undoubtedly the common persimmon, otherwise called *Diospyros virginiana*.

7. *Zamai integrifolia*, commonly called coontie. Laudonnière later told of commerce which existed in the pinelands of south Florida, based upon this valuable plant. It was scarce in the Fort Caroline area where Laudonnière lived, hence was not relied upon except in an emergency. It is a member of the cycad family, one of the oldest forms of plant life on earth. The fern-like plant is now used principally for landscaping; but its roots were used for flour production on a commercial basis as late as 1925, and it was considered an important aid in the feeding of soldiers gassed in World War I. See John Fix, "When Coontie was King," *Florida Wildlife*, December, 1967.

8. The carolina parakeet, *Conuropsis carolinensis*, now extinct.

9. The passenger pigeon, *Ectopistes migratorious*, now extinct.

10. He referred to alligators, which were prevalent in the area and still exist in the river there. The sixteenth-century Spanish explorers called these saurians "lizards," and their phrase for the lizard, *el lagarto*, was the source of the present word "alligator." See *The Oxford English Dictionary*, 1960, 235. A few crocodiles do live in the southern tip of Florida.

11. He referred to the cougar or mountain lion, *Felis concolor*, previously mentioned in the text as the "panther," this being the popular local name for the animal in Florida today. There are somewhere between 100 and 300 such animals still in the wilds in Florida today, according to M. G. Hornocker, "Stalking the Mountain Lion—to Save Him," *National Geographic*, November, 1969.

12. Laudonnière's account of the events of the French settlements in our land was primarily a report rather than a plea for future settlement efforts. Hence, it is understandable that he did not list natural resources in quite the categorical manner used by Thomas Hariot in the latter's colonization plea to the English people to settle Virginia two decades later. See Stefan Lorant, *The New World*, rev. ed. (New York: Duell, Sloan, and Pearce, 1965), 230 ff. Yet the French governor did give his readers a wealth of information on the natural resources of America, and he outlined his persistent and successful efforts to find precious metals and other valuable items of trade.

It is important to note Laudonnière's success in finding gold and other precious items, because to find such things was a primary purpose of the colony. It is reported in Jacques Le Moyne's account of the French in Florida that they ascertained that gold, silver, and copper were mined by the Indians in northern Georgia and southern North Carolina, and the location is so shown on Le Moyne's map in the vicinity of the waterfall shown on the map and in the Le Moyne mining picture in Bennett, *Settlement of Florida* (Gainesville: University of Florida Press, 1968), 3, 85. Other references to such natural resources are on 2, 84, 95, 108. This area in northern Georgia and southwestern North Carolina was the principal source of domestic gold in the United States for minting coins and other purposes prior to the California gold rush of 1849. See A. M. Bateman, *Economic Mineral Deposits* (New York: John Wiley & Sons, 1942), 419.

Laudonnière reported numerous finding of pearls; and Le Moyne stated that one of the French exploratory expeditions reached the Appalachian Mountains to bring back to Fort Caroline gold, silver, emeralds, and sapphires (*Settlement of Florida*, 101, 102). One of the gold-seeking expeditions sent out from Fort Caroline lasted five or six months and another lasted about two months (see pp. 95, 115 below). Each of these accurately established that gold was mined in those mountains, and the French reported how the gold was mined. A goldsmith on the third voyage definitely established, by a testing made in Florida, that the metal from these mountains which was believed to be copper was in fact gold (p. 157 below). See also George F. Becker, "Gold Fields of the Southern Appalachians," in *Sixteenth Annual Report of the United States Geological Survey* (Washington: Government Printing Office, 1894), 251.

Although further examination of documents might disprove the claim of its being the first, it can be reasonably asserted that Laudonnière's expedition to the Appalachians, headed by La Roche Ferrière (*Settlement of Florida*, 84, 99) marked the first taking of gold from the earth by Europeans in what is now the United States. As can be noted from Laudonnière's report, he ascribed great significance to these discoveries and gave consideration to settling Frenchmen in the mining area for the purpose of exploiting this natural resource. The Spanish conquest of Fort Caroline prevented this (*Settlement of Florida*, 108). See also H. B. C. Nitze, "History of Gold Mining in Southern States," in *Twentieth Annual Report of the United States Geological Survey* (Washington: Government Printing Office, 1899), 111; see also other authorities cited in Charles E. Bennett, *Laudonnière and Fort Caroline* (Gainesville: University of Florida Press, 1964), 60n15.

13. Laudonnière referred to "esquine," now chinaroot, or technically *Smilax tammoides*. The roots of other related plants were also used as a cure for syphilis or ulcers: wild sarsaparilla or *Smilax galuca*, and China brier or *Bona-nor hastata*. Syphilis is commonly believed to have originated among the Indians of America and to have been spread throughout Europe by early explorers as they returned to their native lands. See *Encyclopedia Britannica* (Chicago: Benton, 1956), 23:43.

14. See Appendix D for data on plants used by the Indians for dyes and paints.

15. See Appendix D for data on plants used for drugs.

16. Although Laudonnière referred to a large number of these

people among the Indians, it may be questioned that he had the knowledge to pass on such a physiological matter. It seems possible, at least, that these persons were just males who for one reason or another were not warriors and instead did the usual work of Indian women.

17. Three types of holly that grew in the area can be used for a sort of tea, namely: *Ilex vomitoria*, commonly called cassena, which was the Indians' favorite; *Ilex cassine*; and *Ilex glabra*, commonly called inkberry.

18. See Appendix D for data on plants used as foods.

19. Cape François was also mentioned in the account of the second voyage (see p. 59 below). From Laudonnière's account it was apparently a little north of St. Augustine, but Le Moyne placed it just south of St. Augustine in his first picture and on his map. Lowery placed it just above St. Augustine and discussed alternatives (Woodbury Lowery, *The Spanish Settlements within the Present Limits of the United States: Florida, 1562–1574* [New York: Russell & Russell, 1959]), 32.

20. This column stood in Florida until the Spanish conquered the area in 1565. No trace of it has ever been found. Perhaps it was shipped to Spain. A replica of it was erected in 1924 at Mayport by the Florida Daughters of the American Revolution. It has been moved to St. Johns Bluff, where it now stands in the area maintained as the Fort Caroline National Memorial.

21. The St. Johns River, called by the French the River of May.

22. Although it cannot be said with certainty in every case which rivers of today were the rivers named by Laudonnière, this river was probably today's St. Marys River.

23. Satilla River.

24. Turtle River.

25. Altamaha River.

26. Newport River.

27. Medway River.

28. Ogeechee River.

29. Savannah River.

30. The Jordan River was probably the present-day Pee Dee River and was named by Ayllón in 1526 after the captain of one of his vessels. Negro slaves were introduced into the territory, now the United States, by this voyage of 1526; also the first abolitionist reformer to such lands was aboard. See Woodbury

Lowery, *The Spanish Settlements within the Present Limits of the United States, 1513–1561* (New York: Russell & Russell, 1959), 165.

31. Callibogue Sound.

32. Port Royal Sound still bears this name.

33. Laudonnière used here a term, *lentisque*, generally applying to bushes and trees with aromatic gums.

34. Shrimp.

35. Cape Wolf was apparently the westernmost point of Horse Island which was north of Parris Island, separated from it by an indistinct creek. See the Le Moyne map and Appendix C of Ribaut, *Whole and True Discouerye*, 114, where there is a modern map of Parris Island and environs.

36. This pillar was one of five such pillars. One was erected on the banks of the St. Johns in Florida, and one was erected at Port Royal in what is now South Carolina. Three were taken back to France. See Bennett, *Laudonnière*, 119. The one erected at Port Royal was probably set up on Lemon Island on the south side of Broad River, later being sent to Spain by the Spanish who took it in 1564. See Ribaut, *Whole and True Discouerye*, 1927, 109.

37. See note 36, above, for the location of the column.

38. See note 35, above, for the location of the island around which the Liborne River flowed.

39. Perhaps this was Pinckney Island. See map in Ribaut, *Whole and True Discouerye*, 1927, 114.

40. A similar account of a land of rich Indians persisted for years concerning the legend of the wealthy cities of Cibola, which were believed to be in what is now the western United States. See *World Book Encyclopedia* (Chicago: Field Enterprises, 1964), 4:4. Richard Hakluyt in his English version of Laudonnière's account has this notation concerning Chiquola: "This seemeth to be La grand Copal." See Hakluyt, *Voyages* (Edinburgh: Goldsmid, 1889), 13:425. Paul Quattlebaum in *The Land Called Chicora* (Gainesville: University of Florida Press, 1956), 49, gives us an interesting discussion of this area.

41. The site selected was on present-day Parris Island, S.C. See Quattlebaum, *Land Called Chicora*, 49.

42. Jean Ribault said 30 were left there. See Ribaut, *Whole and True Discouerye*, 96. One who remained in America, Guillaume Rouffi, said there were only 26. See Bennett, *Laudonnière*,

119. He also said that 3 died in America and 22 went on the journey back to France.

43. One toise equals 6.396 U.S. feet. Thus the fort was 102.336 feet by 83.148 feet.

44. His full name was Albert de la Pierria. See Ribaut, *Whole and True Discouerye*, 1927, 97.

45. The little creek on Parris Island that flows into Beaufort River.

46. The English translation would be "Shoal River."

47. "Oade," the name of the chief, applied also to his lands along the coast of Georgia. The Spanish later rendered it in their spelling as "Guale," and they applied the name even as far south as Amelia Island, Fla. See Lowery, *Spanish Settlements: Florida*, 347, for a discussion of the location of the Spanish mission of Guale on the coast of Georgia.

48. The Ogeechee River.

49. Laudonnière used the term *almadie* to denote a small Indian boat, evidently distinguished from a canoe, which he defined as being made of one piece of wood, spelling it *canoa*. See p. 116-17 below.

50. The extensive inland passage along the east coast of the United States, which in its improved condition we know today as the intracoastal waterway. See H. O. Locher, *Waterways of the United States* (New York: National Association of River and Harbor Contractors, 1963), 39.

51. Laudonnière later referred to him as Nicolas Masson. See footnote 89.

52. This boat was the first American-built boat to cross the Atlantic Ocean. The journey was perhaps the most horrible voyage of all history.

53. Richard Hakluyt mentioned that Laudonnière apparently referred here to the voyage intended by Stukeley. See Hakluyt, *Voyages*, 13:411; and Bennett, *Settlement of Florida*, xiv, 131, 137, 138.

54. The Treaty of Amboise was signed in March, 1563.

55. Laudonnière stated that the expedition was originally to give succor to the Charlesfort settlement; but by March, 1564, a month before Laudonnière set out from France, the survivors of that settlement had returned to France and had been imprisoned because of the death of Captain Albert. One of them

came to Florida with Laudonnière. See Bennett, *Laudonnière,* 94, 97, 107, 120.

56. The original French text referred to these natives as Indians. See the facsimile edition (1946) of René Laudonnière, *L'Histoire notable* (Paris: Auvray, 1586), 33. But the aboriginal inhabitants of Tenerife, off the coast of Africa, were of course not Indians. They were Guanches, now extinct as a distinct people, being an offshoot of the Berbers of northern Africa. They were of the Cro-Magnon type. They wore garments of goat skin, painted their bodies, manufactured rough pottery, lived in caves and small huts, and used stone implements. See *Encyclopedia Britannica,* 1956, 10:931.

57. The River of Dolphins was what is now the harbor of St. Augustine, Fla., today called Matanzas Inlet.

58. The mount was St. Johns Bluff.

59. Laudonnière's statement merely indicated the northerly direction of his view by mentioning the Belle River. But the argument could be made that the Belle River was to be found at the short distance he mentioned. In that case we would have to assume that he also named Belle River the one we today call the Nassau River. This seems improbable.

60. Although the word *Thimogona* or "Timucuan" with its various spelling has been used to denote the sixteenth-century Indians of northeast Florida, the word was used by those early Indians to describe not themselves but the enemy Indians of the area.

61. June 29, 1564.

62. A portion of the Vale of Laudonnière has not been eroded by the St. Johns River, and in it Fort Caroline has been reconstructed.

63. June 30, 1564. 64. July 28, 1564.

65. Le Moyne's map apparently places Outina's headquarters at Lake Kerr, just west of Lake George.

66. This chief's lands embraced what today is Fort George Island; other portions of the text make him seem the same person as Satouriona.

67. A recently discovered letter of 1563 about Captain Bourdet was translated in Bennett, *Settlement of Florida,* 129.

68. See note 12, above, for the course of this expedition.

69. November 10, 1564.

70. Since Laudonnière is not our only source of information about the Fort Caroline mutinies, it is helpful for the greatest accuracy to consider all other available knowledge. Looking at all known sources, we can state the course of the mutinies with reasonable clarity.

On November 3, 1564, the first group of mutineers left Fort Caroline. Laudonnière said the group consisted of 13 men in a barque. Robert Meleneche, one of these mutineers, and Stefano de Rojomonte, one of a later mutiny, both said the number of this first group was 11. The Meleneche and Rojomonte depositions are in Bennett, *Laudonnière*, 87, 94.

Meleneche stated that these 11 men arrived at Cuba, near a small hamlet named Havana (not to be confused with the city of that name), captured a small boat there, and plundered the village. They then proceeded westward, seeking the port of Matanzas along the northern coast of Cuba, with the master of the captured vessel as a prisoner. They missed their objective and put into a small port named Arcos, near the city of Havana, to get fresh water. Thereupon the prisoner escaped and arranged their capture by two vessels sent from the nearby city of Havana. One of these captured mutineers was François Jean.

Laudonnière reported that 2 Flemish carpenters left Fort Caroline at about the same time as Meleneche's group, but no other information is available as to what happened to them.

Laudonnière reported that on December 8, 1564, the large mutiny of 66 men was under way, with the departure from Fort Caroline of 2 barques which took different courses, one going first to the Bahamas and the other going down the coast, directly to Haiti. Rojomonte was one of the mutineers going first to the Bahamas, and he reported that the 2 groups were never reunited after their splitting up shortly after leaving Fort Caroline.

Rojomonte's barque eventually went to Cape San Nicolás on the northern peninsula on the western shore of Haiti, and captured a boat near there before coming into the vicinity of the city of Havana, where they were themselves captured.

The other barque of the December mutiny was piloted by Trenchant and went to Arcahaie on the center of the western coast of Haiti, captured a brigantine there, and engaged in a bloody battle with the inhabitants of Arcahaie. Thence they sailed to the Cape of Santa María (near their original objective of

Leauguave). There on the northern tip of the southern peninsula of Haiti they repaired their captured brigantine.

Then they sailed to Baracoa, a port on the eastern tip of Cuba (erroneously thought by Laudonnière to be in Jamaica). They captured a 60-ton caravel there and pillaged the city. Then they took the caravel to the Cape of Tiburon on the southern tip of the southern peninsula of Haiti. In the neighborhood of that cape they captured a small Spanish vessel with 12 aboard, including a magistrate, called a "governor" by Laudonnière.

Francisco Ruiz Manso, the pilot of the Spanish boat carrying the magistrate, was captured by the French and later told the story of this capture, and of what followed, in a deposition to be found in Bennett, *Laudonnière*, 103. Manso explained how the French were tricked into danger at Jamaica, where they sought supplies and received instead such vigorous combat that most of the French were captured.

Those Frenchmen who escaped from this adventure made their way northward from Jamaica and around the western tip of Cuba, thence eastward past Havana and northward to Fort Caroline. The story of their punishment is discussed by Laudonnière in his account, and also by Jacques Le Moyne.

Juan Rodríguez de Noriega wrote Philip II on March 29, 1565, that, on the basis of information secured from Spanish-captured French mutineers, it would be wise and proper to wipe the French out of Florida without delay.

Pedro Menéndez de Avilés wrote to Philip II on September 11, 1565, that he had 3 of the captured mutineers with him when he left Sapin for Florida. One of these mutineers was the François Jean who led Menéndez to Fort Caroline. See note 71, below, and Bennett, *Settlement of Florida*, 148.

71. Laudonnière never clearly identified this mischief, but he is probably making reference to the fact that one of these mutineers, François Jean, later led Menéndez to Fort Caroline. Hakluyt, *Voyages*, had at this point a marginal notation: "One of these mariners, named Francis Jean, betrayed his own countrymen to the Spaniard and brought them into Florida."

72. That is, South America.

73. This statement by Laudonniére as to his orders, and his firm punishment of the mutineer pirates, speak eloquently to deny that Fort Caroline was planned as a base for piracy.

74. Jacques Le Moyne stated that Laudonnière was in fetters. See Bennett, *Settlement of Florida*, 100.

75. On the southern peninsula of Haiti.

76. In fact, they never were rejoined.

77. Arcahaie, Haiti.

78. Baracoa was, and is today, on the eastern tip of Cuba. Laudonnière made a mistake by locating the village in Jamaica.

79. On the southwestern tip of the southern peninsula of Haiti.

80. The title of this man was not as high as Laudonnière indicated. He was a judge or magistrate. See note 70 above.

81. The village was probably Villa de la Vega, then the capital of the island. It is near the present-day capital city of Kingston and is called Spanish Town.

82. Western tip of Cuba.

83. Ribault Bay, now the harbor of the Mayport Naval Station.

84. South Florida.

85. The Florida Keys.

86. Hakluyt has a marginal notation at this point: "One of the Spaniards was named Martin Gomes."

87. Lake Okeechobee.

88. In south Florida.

89. Hakluyt has a marginal notation at this point: "Nicolas Masson otherwise called Nicolas Barre." See footnote 51.

90. Lake George.

91. Perhaps Flemings Island near Green Cove Springs, Fla.

92. Sorrel, more technically called *verticillatus* or *pulcher*.

93. August 8, 1565.

94. *Pinocqs* were water chinquapens, more technically named *Nelumbo lutea*.

95. We are indebted to Mary Ross for an account of a similar Indian ruse that resulted in a Spanish tragedy. It was in 1576 when a Spanish patrol in South Carolina was met in a village by a crafty chief who objected to the unfriendly and warlike appearance of lighted tapers. When they were quenched, all of the Spaniards but one were killed by the Indians. The one who escaped told the story. See Mary Ross, "French Intrusions and Indian Uprisings in Georgia and South Carolina (1577–1580)," *Georgia Historical Quarterly* (September, 1923), 7:251.

96. Fort Caroline's artist Jacques Le Moyne was one of those injured. Hakluyt has a marginal notation to this effect, and it is evident from Le Moyne's own statement that he was on this

expedition and was convalescing from wounds at the time of the fall of Fort Caroline. See Bennett, *Settlement of Florida*, 68, 114. See also the further statement by Laudonnière that those who were convalescing at the time of the fall of Fort Carolina were recovering from wounds received in the battle against Outina's forces (p. 163, below).

97. This statement is indicative of Laudonniére's writing being in progress soon after his return to France.

98. This comment is reminiscent of the comment your translator often heard from the lips of the late Speaker Sam Rayburn: "It takes a carpenter to build a barn, but any jackass can kick one down."

99. Thus St. Augustine, the oldest city in the United States, began.

100. Captain la Grange drowned when Ribault's fleet sank. See Bennett, *Settlement of Florida*, 114.

101. Le Challeux, author of *Last Voyage of Ribaut*.

102. Son of Jean Ribault.

103. For details concerning Laudonnière's reporting to the king see Lowery, *Spanish Settlements: Florida*, 314.

Notes to Appendix B

1. Those shareholders having between them a third interest in the vessel's cargo.

2. In "Les Collectionneurs de bêtes sauvages, 1047–1572," *Bulletin du Musée d'Histoire Naturelle*, 1902, 242.

3. "Le Capitaine René de Laudonnière—Nouveaux renseignements sur ses navigations, 1561–1572," *Bulletin de géographie historique et descriptive*, 1902.

4. He had not sailed at the time of the St. Bartholomew's Day massacre, nor during the following days. That he had not sailed would seem certain because in September, 1572, he appeared before a notary in Saint-Germain-en-Laye. In that month he was also involved there in a lawsuit before the Table du Marbre between Claude Pacquelon, a son of Jean, and "René de Laudonnière, ship's captain living at Saint-Germain-en-Laye." See Archives Nationales, Paris, File Z-LdI, fol. 28. A copy of these court Proceedings is at the Fort Caroline National Memorial. Some scholars think that Laudonnière was scheduled to go on a mysterious mis-

sion in 1573, which fell through, and we do know certainly that Laudonnière died at Saint-Germain-en-Laye on July 24, 1574. See Charles E. Bennett, "A Footnote on René Laudonnière," *Florida Historical Quarterly* (January, 1967), 45:289.

5. This was the deep water roadstead sheltered by the islands of Ré and Oleron, near the harbor of La Pallice, where the royal fleets and trading fleets of the region had assembled from time immemorial.

6. *Tiercements.*

7. Connor observes in a marginal notation: "The last third is divided into sixteenths, but it seems impossible to apportion them among these names, unless it is meant that 'the said sieurs de la Fons and Fautrel' were each responsible for one-quarter or four-sixteenths."

8. It was thus that the West Indies and the mainland were designated. See Ch. and P. Bréard, *Documents relatifs à la Marine Normande et à ses armements aux XVIe et XVIIe siècles pour le Canada, l'Afrique, les Antilles, le Brézil et les Indes* (Rouen, 1889), 145–48.

9. The amount assessed in proportion to their respective interests against each consignee and the owners of the vessel so as to cover the loss to ship or cargo.

10. A livre, before the French Revolution, was nearly equivalent to a franc. It contained 20 sous (solz).

11. Said in ancient times of any money coined in the city of Tours.

12. "This profit is very high. In the middle of the XVI century, the rate of interest for [voyages to] Newfoundland does not seem to have exceeded 40 per cent; it is true that the voyage to Peru made one run more risk," G. Musset, "Les Rochelais à Terre-Neuve," *Bulletin de géographie du Comité des Travaux Historiques et Scientifiques*, 1892, 268. According to the Bréards the interest then mounted as high, sometimes, as 55 per cent.

13. So the members of the crew were forbidden to trade with the natives, with the articles they might each have brought in their personal baggage, until the captain or master of the ship acting for the enterprise had finished negotiations with the natives and had given his consent thereto.

14. Cabin boys.

Index

Acorns: a part of diet of Indians and French, 123; picture of, by Le Moyne, 126

Albert [de la Pierria], Captain: left in charge at Charlesfort, 33n44; assassinated, 47

Alligators: called crocodiles, 9n10, 45

Arlac. *See* d'Arlac

Athore: a place where Frenchmen were killed, 132

Atinas, Martin: Frenchmen with Hawkins who was also on 1562 trip, 142

Atore: son of Satouriona, 61; at Somme River, 140

Audusta: Indian king at Charlesfort, 38; friendly to French, 39; allowed French to observe toya celebrations, 40; assisted in rebuilding Charlesfort, 44–45; assisted in building boat for return to France from Charlesport, 48; visited by Vasseur in 1565, 113; sent food to Laudonnière, 113–14

Aymon: Frenchman who was on both 1562 and 1564 voyages, 113

Barré, Captain Nicolas: elected leader at Charlesfort, 47; also called Nicolas Mason, 47n51, 113n89

Basse River: visited on 1562 voyage, 37n46

Belle à Veoir River: visited on 1562 voyage, 23; name for Callibogue Sound, 23n31

Belle River: visited on 1562 voyage, 22, 43; name for Ogeechee River, 22n28, 43n59

Baurdet, Captain: come to Caroline Sept. 4, 1564, 95; returned to France Nov. 10, 1564, 96

Calos: Indian king of South Florida who claimed Godlike abilities, 110–12

Canaveral, Cape: home of Oathchagua 112

Caroline: construction of fort begun with prayer, 70; description of construction, 72–73; named "la Caroline" after Charles IX, king of France, 73; second voyage ships returned to France, July 28, 1564, 82; clay for brick and mortar at, 96; famine at, May-June 1565, 121–22; extreme famine conditions at, 130; picture of, 150; rebuilt in 1565, 162; captured by Spanish, 163–65

Catherine de Medeci: approved St. Bartholomew's Day massacre, xxi; Laudonnière served under, xxii; portrait of, 57

Cedars, Isle of: visited in 1562, 27

Charente River: visited on 1562 voyage, 22; name for Altamaha River, 22n25

Charles IX, king of France: Charles-

227

fort named for, xiv, 36; approved St. Bartholomew's Day massacre, xxi; ordered the 1564 expedition, 53; portrait of, 54; Caroline named for, 73; glass pictures of him given as trinkets to Indians, 88; Laudonnière reported to, 169

Charlesfort: settled in 1562, xiii, 35–36; named for Charles IX, xiv, 36; location 35; burned and rebuilt, 44; discord and mutiny at, 46–47; settlers built ship to return to France, 47–48;; settlers used moss and resin to caulk ship, 48; settlers drank their urine and indulged in cannibalism on return trip, 49–50; survivors reached England, 50–51

Chiquola: Indian king, 29–30n40

Coligny, Gaspard de, admiral of France: chose Ribault to command 1562 expedition, xiv, 17; as French leader, xvii; chose Laudonnière to command 1564 expedition, xvii, 53–55; decided to reinforce Caroline, xvii; murdered in St. Bartholomew's Day massacre, xxi; portrait of, 19; asked succor for Charlesfort, 53; sent message to Laudonnière, 154

Copper: mined in Appalachian Mountains, given to Laudonnière by Indians, 116

Crocodiles. See Alligators

Cypress trees: at Charlesfort area, 45

D'Arlac: Laudonnière's ensign, 59, 88; called lord, 88; sent to live with Outina, 88; returned to Caroline, 92; managed plank preparation for shipbuilding, 123; in combat with Outina's forces, 137–39

De Hais, Jean: master carpenter, 140; helped Laudonnière escape, 165

De la Vigne: in charge at the time of attack on Caroline, 163

Dolphins, River of: so named by Laudonnière, 60; name of Matanzas Inlet, harbor of St. Augustine, 60n57; Menéndez arrived there, 158; also called Seloy River, 158

D'Ottigni: Laudonnière's lieutenant, 58; reconnoitered with Laudonnière, 59; sent to reconnoiter Indans, 62; assisted by Indians on trip, 63; observed very old Indian, 64; sent to visit the Thimogona, 73–75; called captain, 75; assisted Outina in defeating Potavou, 117–21; ordered to get timber for ship construction, 123; sent to Outina's village for food, 135; in battle with Outina's forces, 137–39; counseled with sick Laudonnière, 159

Du Lys, Lord: left in charge at Caroline by Ribault, 160; assisted Laudonnière, 161

Durand, Nicolas, lord of Villegagnon: built Fort Coligny in 1555, in Brazil, xv; portrait of, 10

Edelano, Island of: in St. John's River (River of May), 115; Pierre Gambye on, 116–17

Ferrière, La Roche: sent on six-months reconnaissance in Indian country, 95; visited Houstaqua, 95–96

Fish: kinds of, 20, 24; methods of fishing, 20, 23–24

Fourneaux: mutineer, 97

France: claims to occupancy of America, xv

François, Cape: on Florida coast, 59

Gambye, Pierre: stayed at Edelano on the way to the gold mines, 116; collected gold and silver, 116; murdered, 117

Garonne River: visited on 1562 voyage, 22; name for Newport River, 22n26

Genre: a mutineer, 92; confidant of Laudonnièrre, 92–93; sought to kill Laudonnière, 93; accused and banished, 95–96

Gironde River: visited on 1562 voyage, 22; name for Medway River, 22n27

Gold: in America, 9; used in Indian armor, 77; Molano promised large quantities of, 77; reconnaissance brought back gold, 92; gold plates as Indian ornamentation, 110; mines in Apalachian Mountains, 5 or 6 days' distance from Caroline, 116; Indian methods of mining, 116; to be scught further in Appalachian Mountains, 157; metal identified as gold found in Appalachian Mountains, 157

Grande River: visited on 1562 voyage, 22; name for Savannah River, 22n29

Grotauld: explored two months in Indian country, 115–16; visited Houstaqua, 116; brought back copper, 116

Hais: Jean de. *See* De Hais, Jean

Hance, Master: keeper of munitions, 123

Hawkins, Captain John: visited Caroline, xvii, 141–45; arrived Aug. 3, 1565; generosity of, 143–45

Hermaphrodites: one assisted the French, 70; were food-carriers in battle, 117

Houstaqua: Indian king, 77; received La Roche Ferrière, 95; sent gifts to Laudonnière, 95–96; his area commanded the route to the mountains, 116; had 3,000 to 4,000 warriors, 116; knew the location of the gold mines, 116

Indians: description and customs, 9–16; combat among, 11; celebrations, 11; games, 11–12; marriage, 13; syphillis among, 13; hermaphrodites and Sodomites among, 13; religion, 13–15; priests-doctors, 13, 15; food, 13, 15–16, 187–209; use of cassena drink, 14; burials, 14; agriculture, 15; medical treatment, 16; used weirs in fishing, 20; used mulberries, 20; trinkets given to, 20–21; corn a staple among, 20, 42; traded deerskins, baskets, pearls, 26; some taken captive at Port Royal, 28; customs in eating, 29; used acorns and roots as food, 42; beans a staple among, 42; traded in pearls, crystal, and silver ore, 46; gifts by them of silver, 61, 67, 92, 96; Laudonnière praised their artistic ability, 62; guarded their cornfields, 62; Indians of great age, 64, 65; gave red and blue gourds, 65; Indian arrows compared unfavorably with French guns, 67; ceremonies in celebration of victory, 79–92; ceremonies in preparation for battle, 83; celebration after a victory, 85; custom of retiring to the woods during January, February, and March, 121; traded cleverly with French during famine, 124; Outina's followers asked that French fuses be extinguished, 135n95; entertained Frenchmen at Somme River in 1565, 140

Inland Passage: intracoastal waterway, 45n50

Jarua: a magician-priest, foretold positions of enemy, 120

Jean, François: betrayed Laudonnière, 164

Joana: a priest, 41

Jordan River: referred to, 22, 24; name for the Pee Dee River, 22n30

La Caille, François: sergeant of Laudonnière, 78; presented plea of mutineers, 98

La Croix: mutineer, 97

La Grange, Captain, visited sick Laudonnière, 159; sided with Laudonnière in dispute with Ribault, 161

Laudonnière, Captain René: portrait of, frontispiece, 71; on 1562 expedition to America as second in command, xiii; commanded 1864 expedition, xvi; birth, xvi; commanded ship *Le Chien* in 1561, xvii; on voyage to Algiers in 1561, xvii; returned to Europe in 1565, xix, 168; wrote an account of the three voyages, xix-xx; appeared before Charles IX at Moulins, xxi, 169; employed by Cardinal of Bourbon as captain of

Countess Testu, xxi; a Protestant, xxi; contracted for another American voyage in 1572, xxi; escaped St. Bartholomew's Day massacre in 1572, xxi; captain of the Western Fleet in 1573, xxi; resident of Saint- Germain-en-Laye, xxii, death, xxii; served various monarchs of France, xxii; evaluation, xxii; gave his reasons for foreign settlements, 4–6; described boundaries and parts of New World, 6–8; described New France, 8; described American plant life, 8, 9, 23–24; described American animal life, 9, 15, 23; located gold resources in Appalachian Mountains, 9; described Indians, 9–10; learned Indian language, 29; helped plan Charlesfort, 35; said, "God, who knows the hearts and minds of men, never forsakes those who need Him," 44; said, "misfortune, or more accurately the judgment of God, decreed that those who could not even be over come by fire and water could nevertheless destroy themselves. It is common among men that they cannot tolerate living without change, and would rather ruin themselves than be deprived of something every day," 46; said, "necessity teaches everything," 47-48; chosen by Coligny to lead the 1564 expedition, 53; described the 1564 voyage to America, 55–56; visited Mayport column on June 25, 1564, 61; said of St. Johns Bluff," the place is so pleasant that it would force the depressed to lift their spirits," 65; promised to fight the Thimagona, 66; vale under St. Johns Bluff named after him, 69–70; excused himself from promise to fight the Thimagona, 82–83; had troubles with Satouriona over prisoners, 86; got foodstuffs from Sautouriona, 87; urged Satouriona to fight Onatheaqua rather than Outina, 87; pretended a fire by lightning was his doing, 89; plot to kill him by poison or explosion, 93–94; ill on September 20, 1564, 93; said, "Greed . . . the mother of all mischief," 97; illness of, 99; confined by mutineers for 15 days, 100; signed passport under duress, 100; sent Ottigny to help Outina defeat Potavou to open way for French to get to gold mines, 117; led expedition to collect food, 123; led expedition to seize Outina and son, to punish Indians, and to collect food, 127–28; returned to Outina's village to collect food and return Outina's son, 133; second return to Outina's village to collect food, 134; appraised his efforts in America, 141; refused to give Hawkins treasures, 144; planned to take Indians back to France, 146; said, "the character of good men is often attacked by people who, not having earned credit themselves, try to tear down the work of others, hoping by this to strengthen their own weak courage," 151–52; refused to stay on after Ribault's arrival at Caroline, 154; received letter from Coligny, 154; criticized in France for bringing unmarried women on trip, 154–55; said, "a governor must make himself understood and must lead, otherwise everyone would see himself as in charge," 155; answered various criticisms, 155–56; said, "how often misfortune searches us out and pursues us even when we think that everything is going just right," 157; advised Ribault not to fight at sea, 159–61; escaped after fall of Caroline, 165; arrived in England, 168; arrived in London, Calais, Paris, and Moulins, 169; appraises reasons for France's loss of Florida, 169–70

Le Challeux, Nicolas: carpenter at Caroline who wrote an account of his experiences, xviii; mentioned as being at least sixty years of age, 162–63

Le Genevoys, Estienne: mutineer, 97

Le Moyne [de Morgues], Jacques: artist on expedition of 1564 who recorded events in narrative and pictures, xviii

Liborne River: visited in 1562, 27

Loire River: visited on 1562 expedition, 22; name for Turtle River, 22n24

Magnolia: use of, in ceremonies, 20–21; decorated Mayport column, 61; on St. Johns Bluff, 65, 65n58

May, River of (St. Johns River): named for day of discovery, May 1, 1562, 22; Laudonnière landed at, June 25, 1564, 60; selected as site of Caroline, 68–69

Menéndez [de Avilés], Pedro: led Spanish attack on French Florida, xvii; founded St. Augustine, xvii; captured Caroline, xvii, 164; his biography, xvi; arrived at River of May, 157; settled at St. Augustine, 159; led attack on Caroline, 164

Molona: Indian king, 76; received Vasseur, 76; vassal of Outina, 76; named allies and enemies, 76–77; promised alliance by Vasseur, 77

Mutiny: at Charlesfort, 46–47; begun at Caroline, 92; of the Flemish carpenters, 96; of 13 men, 96–97; of 66 men, 98–106; leaders executed, 106

Oade: Indian chief, 42; name also applied to his lands, 42n47; generous to Charlesfort, 44–45

Oathchaqua: Indian king whose daughter was captured, 11–12

Onatheaqua: Indian chief who lived near the mountains, 77

Ottigni. See D'Ottigni

Outina, Olata Ouae: Indian king, 76; enemy of Satouriona, 76; ruled 40 vassal kings, 76; visited by d'Arlac and Vasseur, 91; aided by French in fight against Potavou, 91; asked Laudonnière for more aid against Potavou, 117; picture of, 118; assisted by French in war against Potavou, 119–21; deceived Laudonnière over cause

of war, 125; seized by Laudonnière, 128

Port Royal: named, 23, 36; rejected as site of settlement in 1564, 68

Potavou: Indian king of substance and character, enemy to Outina, 76, 91; his lands commanded the route to the gold mines, 117; conquered by Outina with French help, 117–21

Priests: joanas, 41; jaruas, 119–20

Ribault, Jacques, Laudonnière's difficulties with, 166–67

Ribault, Jean: led 1562 expedition to America, xiii, 17; employed by Henry VIII and Edward VI of England, xiii; French representative to Scotland, xiv; fought with Protestants in France, xvi; fled to England, xvi; planned in England to succor Charlesfort, xvi; imprisoned, xvi; wrote of America, xvi; planned to attack Menéndez' ships, xvii-xviii, 158–61; death of, xviii; erected column at Mayport in 1562, 18; erected column at Port Royal in 1562, 27; challenged Frenchmen to settle America, 31–32; portrait resembling his description, 33; took 1562 expedition back to France, 38; returned to Florida in 1565, 149–41; talked to Laudonnière about reports in France, 153; asked Laudonnière to stay in America, 153; remembered by Indians, 156; warned by Coligny against Spaniards in Florida, 160; departs in search of Spanish ships, 161

Roquette: mutineer, 92

Rouffi: remained at Charlesfort when French left, 113; sought by French, 113; captured by Spanish, 113

St. Augustine: founded by Menédez, xvii

St. Johns Bluff; observed by Laudonnière, 62; vegetation described, 65, 187–209

San Mateo; name given Caroline by Spanish, xvii

Satouriona: king of Indians living near Caroline, 61; aided construction of Caroline, 72; monarch of the valley of the River of May, 76; had 30 vassal chiefs, 76; portrait, 84; went to war with other Indians, 85; collected scalps, 85–86; also called Allicamany, 69n66; urged Laudonnière to fight Outina, 112; asked Laudonnière to give Outina to him, 129–30; came to visit Ribault, 156

Seine River: visited on 1562 expedition, 22; name for St. Marys River, 22n22; visited in 1564, 67

Shipbuilding, 2 large barques, 97; another barque after mutineers departed, 107; a galley, 122; supervised by de Hais, 140

Shrimp: taken by net, 24

Silkworms: found by French, 21

Silver: found in America, 9; used as Indian armor, 77; King Molona promised much to French, 77; given to Laudonnière by Outina, 92

Somme River: visited by 1562 expedition, 22; name for Satilla River, 22n23; visited in 1564, 67

Spain: claimed lands in America, xv-xvi; considered abandoning parts of America, xvi; Laudonnière cautioned not to trespass upon, 109

Spaniards: rescued by French from Indians, 109

Thanksgiving; prayers for safe arrival, 70

Thimogona: name fo Indian enemies, 66; "Timucuan" derived from, 66n60

Toya: a secret Indian ceremony, 29; described, 39–42

Trenchant: pilot assigned by Laudonnière to go with mutineers, 100–101; assisted in negotiations with Hawkins, 145

Vasseur, Captain: sent to search for missing Frenchman, 75–76; taken to King Molona, 76; told by Molona of Indian friends and enemies, 76–77; pretended victory over Molona's enemies, 78; sent to live with Outina, 88, 90–91; sent to get d'Arlac, 92; sent to Audusta, 113–15; sent to aid Outina, 125; sent for food to Somme River in 1565, 139–40; aided in negotiations with Hawkins, 145; assigned to command a ship on return to France, 149

Verdier, Captain, aided in negotiations with Hawkins, 145; assigned to command a ship on return to France, 149